Restored by the Storm

ENDORSEMENTS

I have been truly honored in my lifetime to connect with people that have a true calling, and a gift to help people. Bill has both, as well as a life journey that you will find in his book *Restored by The Storm*. He shows that with faith and the right attitude, tough times can be a tremendous blessing. You will be captivated by his story and the lessons learned during this time in his life, and it will inspire those who are going through similar storms in their life. A definite read that you won't want to put down until you have completed it.

— **Bryan Dodge**, National Professional Development Speaker/Coach, author of the *Good Life Rules*, *Becoming the Obvious Choice, The Principles of Unstoppable Family Business.*

In *Restored by The Storm*, Bill Derrick masterfully encapsulates the essence of resilience, faith, and the unanticipated blessings that life's fiercest storms can unveil. This book is not merely a recount of survival; it is a testament to the profound transformation and restoration that comes when we confront our challenges head-on, with faith as our anchor. Derrick's journey through personal upheaval mirrors the unexpected paths many of us find ourselves on, reminding us that amidst the wreckage, there is an opportunity for renewal and growth. For men seeking a beacon of hope and practical wisdom on navigating life's tumultuous seasons, Derrick offers not just a guide but a companion for the journey. His story is a powerful affirmation that with faith, perseverance, and the right attitude, we can emerge from our storms not just intact but improved, restored, and ready to face what comes next with strength and grace.

— **Vince Miller**, Founder & President of Resolute.

Are you in the middle of a storm? Are you looking for hope? This book is exactly what you are looking for. Bill's message is powerful – God will give you the strength to overcome while you are overcoming – not before – for that is when you truly experience the longest 12-inch journey in the world – the journey of your faith moving from your head to your heart and what restoration really means.

— **Tom Ziglar**, CEO Zig Ziglar Corporation

RESTORED
BY THE STORM

Navigating Through
Life's Unexpected Challenges

BILL
DERRICK

NEW YORK

LONDON • NASHVILLE • MELBOURNE • VANCOUVER

RESTORED BY THE STORM

Navigating Through Life's Unexpected Challenges

Unless otherwise noted, Scripture is taken from the HOLY BIBLE, NEW INTERNATIONAL VERSION®. NIV®. Copyright © 1973, 1978, 1984 by International Bible Society. Used by permission of Zondervan. All rights reserved worldwide.

Scripture quotations marked NLT are taken from the Holy Bible, New Living Translation, copyright © 1996, 2004, 2015 by Tyndale House Foundation. Used by permission of Tyndale House Publishers, Inc., Carol Stream, Illinois 60188. All rights reserved.

Scripture quotations marked (ESV) are from The ESV® Bible (The Holy Bible, English Standard Version®), © 2001 by Crossway, a publishing ministry of Good News Publishers. Used by permission. All rights reserved.

Published in New York, New York, by Morgan James Publishing. Morgan James is a trademark of Morgan James, LLC. www.MorganJamesPublishing.com

Proudly distributed by Publishers Group West®

Morgan James BOGO™

A **FREE** ebook edition is available for you or a friend with the purchase of this print book.

CLEARLY SIGN YOUR NAME ABOVE

Instructions to claim your free ebook edition:
1. Visit MorganJamesBOGO.com
2. Sign your name CLEARLY in the space above
3. Complete the form and submit a photo of this entire page
4. You or your friend can download the ebook to your preferred device

ISBN 9781636984254 paperback
ISBN 9781636984261 ebook
Library of Congress Control Number: 2024941118

Cover Design by:
Rachel Lopez
www.r2cdesign.com

Interior Design by:
Chris Treccani
www.3dogcreative.net

Morgan James is a proud partner of Habitat for Humanity Peninsula and Greater Williamsburg. Partners in building since 2006.

Get involved today! Visit: www.morgan-james-publishing.com/giving-back

This book is dedicated to Jeanne, my wife of forty-three years, who has been by my side through the good times as well as the storms in our lives. Her selfless love and encouragement always help to point me in the right direction.

I also dedicate this book to my four children, Michael, Lydia, Wesley, and Shelby, and our current and future grandchildren. May they learn from my story and be inspired to be the best that they can be as they walk through the precious life that God has given them.

CONTENTS

PREFACE

On Friday the 13th of August in 2004, Hurricane Charley unexpectedly came ashore as a major Category 4 storm with its path coming right up Charlotte Harbor in Southwest Florida. The full strength and power of this hurricane were on a path to directly hit Punta Gorda with winds of 149 mph and higher. It was said that the anemometer at the Punta Gorda Airport last measured 160 mph before it broke! Earlier that day, Charley hit Cuba "only" as a Category 2 storm, and its projected path was expected to take it to the Tampa–St. Petersburg area. Instead, and during that dreadful afternoon, Charley did the unexpected as only hurricanes can do. It intensified and made a right-hand turn toward the communities of Punta Gorda and Port Charlotte. Many were caught off guard as they found themselves riding out one of the most powerful hurricanes to ever hit Florida—even to this day.

Destruction was absolutely everywhere!

Mobile home communities were reduced to rubble. Beautiful homes in the canal communities had their roofs ripped off, pools filled with debris, and windows blown out. Downtown was in shambles and looked like a war zone, with severe damage and debris strewn all over the place. In the end, fifteen lives were lost and billions of dollars' worth of damage was inflicted on the surrounding communities. This unexpected storm, that hit in an unexpected place with unexpected intensity, completely devastated the area.

I remember visiting Punta Gorda five months after the storm, and there was still widespread, massive devastation. Where there used to be a business, there was now a windswept empty lot. Streets that went through mobile home communities still had ten-foot-high "windrows" of rubble on the side of the street, all waiting to be hauled away to the debris mountain south on Hwy 41. Homes were missing most of the concrete tiles from their roofs. Pool cages and screens ripped off their lanais and deposited God knows where. Charley had destroyed so much of the city—but it didn't destroy the spirit of those who lived there or called it home during the winter. The city immediately started the long process of rebuilding. Today, some twenty years later, you would never know that a massive hurricane with so much destructive power ever came through here. Punta Gorda is now more beautiful than ever. Yes, remnants of the storm remain, but those areas serve as a memorial to those who were there on that fateful day.

Restored by the storm.

Okay, the storm itself didn't restore anything, but the spirit and hard work of the people who live here restored it to a level above and beyond the original version.

And then almost eighteen years later, Hurricane Ian, a much larger and powerful storm, devastated much of the same southwest coast of Florida from Naples to Venice. As you flew into Fort Myers after this major storm, you could look down and see the devastation along what used to be pristine beaches and coastline. There were blue tarps on roofs everywhere. Large boats were underwater in the marinas. Once again, tragedy struck this area, and once again the people of Southwest Florida are building back. There is no doubt it will be restored, perhaps even better in some areas. It will be different, but it will be restored.

I have taken to documenting my story in much the same manner. My story is that of the unexpected, the gut-wrenching "drive you to your knees" personal storms that I have recently experienced, and the rebuilding effort afterward. You see, these storms were never supposed to happen, as far as I was concerned. I was one of those lucky ones who had his wonderful life all planned out in a specific order and under control. Yes, we had "storms," but life was good, as they say, and we were able to escape those major storms. Business was good. It was growing year after year, and we were living a great life. We were comfortable, successful, busy, having fun, and seemingly in control. Then, as life does to so many of us, the rug was pulled out from under me. I guess God didn't necessarily think that I was following the right plan—at least not in a way he wanted. I believe that sometimes when we tell God our plans, he just smiles and lets us continue down the road to our demise.

But others, like me, are fortunate to have God get our attention. In my case I believe that a tap on the shoulder would've sufficed, but God decided to really get my attention and figuratively hit me upside the head with a 2 x 6 (yes, I am in the construction business). It started with the Great Recession when I found out that I and our family business had no immunity to serious adversity.

So, my question became, What was the purpose of this storm? Why take a perfectly good life and turn it upside down?

I have come to realize that the storms we face come as unwanted gifts from God. Most of us are familiar with the white elephant gift exchange sometimes done at the holidays. Have you ever had the experience of getting stuck with something you perceived to be junk at the time? Then inevitably you found out it does have some value and you end up finding the perfect use for it. Pain, stress, hurt, headaches, and sleepless nights can all be a part of going through a personal storm. I don't believe that God wants us to hurt or be hurt, but he does want our attention. God uses our storms to teach us, strengthen our faith, and change us for the better. These experiences can change our attitude toward life and, most importantly, toward the loved ones we care about. It's not the story of the storm that is so important, nor is it how we finally escape it, rather it's how we deal with the adversity and what we learn from the experience. This is how we are restored better, stronger, and more able-bodied than ever before, and certainly different.

I believe that with the right attitude and with faith that God is always there with us, we will survive any storm thrown our way and, in many cases, fare much better on the other side! Sometimes it takes a while to ride it all out. Sometimes it's merely a glancing blow by a Category 1, and sometimes we are hit by the eye wall of a Category 4! However, it does pass, and then we have a chance to improve as we pick up the debris and rebuild. There is never any guarantee that another storm won't strike again, and what we learn from each setback is vitally important.

As I write this, we have just finished the COVID-19 pandemic. Many people have experienced their first significant stretch of misfortune and hard times. I have had this book in my heart for quite some time now and have been encouraged by many of my friends to get it written. Now is the season for me to sit and write. My story is about the major storms that I've had to navigate, how I got through them, and how they changed me. My story is about thinking I had life all figured out only to find out that I didn't. Yet when the wind quit blowing and the waves started to subside, I became closer to God and was able to better see him working with me. I don't intend to preach, but I do hope that you're inspired where you might need inspiration. My story will hopefully bring you hope. If you are stuck in tumultuous waters right now, and many are, hang on, this too shall pass. I sincerely hope that this book is helpful, and I appreciate your coming along on the journey as I recall what seem like the most

significant times of my life—the unexpected storms that drove
me to my knees.

CHAPTER 1:

In Control

Who wouldn't want their life under control? Having life all figured out and unfolding just the way you planned it is the way it should be, right? That's certainly the way I envisioned it. I believed that a normal successful life was not only possible but very doable. All I had to do was plan out what I wanted, set goals, do the right things, and work hard. It was that simple to me. Receiving my engineering degree was the first step to start that journey—as I had dreams of being an executive with a large engineering or construction firm. My ambitions were focused, and I was very resolute, very determined. I was of the mindset that you'd better not stand in the way, because I had the vehicle in high gear, and it was rolling.

Six months before graduating from the University of Minnesota, it happened.

Quite by accident and very unexpectedly, my eyes met the eyes of a coed at a college event, and I truly believe it was love at first sight. Jeanne and I seemed to share so much in common. We enjoyed each other's company, had great conversations, laughed a lot, and were very happy together. But she was an undergraduate and was still working on getting her degree before starting her business career. During this time, I acquired some great experience in heavy and high-rise construction. I spent some quality time in Mississippi, Georgia, and Minnesota, learning as much as I possibly could. I was unsure what God had in mind, but I thoroughly believed he had gifted me with the intelligence, knowledge, and ability to succeed in whatever I did. He expected me to use those endowments for the better, make something of myself, and make great things happen. You see, I believed I was staying close to God in my own way. I was a prayerful and church-going young man wherever I happened to be. It was extremely important for me to stay connected to the church and maintain a high level of spirituality. I was also able to separate my faith life from my work life. To me, it was the wisest way to look at things as a Christian—staying balanced between faith and secular activity. It was all part of the plan, seemed logical, and made total sense.

The attraction to Jeanne ebbed and flowed as she finished her final two years of college and started her business career. At the time, I was living in the South (certainly a culture shock for a country boy from Wisconsin!) and kind of just doing my own thing. We would see each other when I came home for visits, and she visited me a couple of times while I lived in Mississippi. Long-distance relationships can be very hard and challenging, as anybody that has lived through one will attest. Just when we started questioning the wisdom of our affiliation (aren't all strong relationships based on wisdom?), that original spark happened again, and we could no longer deny the love we had for each other. We made the commitment and were married some four years after meeting each other—one of the happiest days of my life, by the way! In retrospect, it's certainly obvious that God had a hand in all this and was guiding and directing us. At the time, we probably saw it more as fate—as our destiny.

We both had great careers and, together, we were starting down the trail toward being financially successful. It was important for us to be able to do whatever we wanted, when we wanted, and not wait until normal retirement age to do it. We were learners and gobbled up all the self-help books we could. We listened to many cassette tapes (dating ourselves?) on how to be successful in sales and business. During the first five years of our marriage, we both thought it would be important to add to our education by getting MBA degrees. We wanted to do this before starting a family. Hard work was very important to us, and we believed that this would take us where we wanted to go. Therefore, many of our nights were spent either in class (I was at the University of Minnesota, and she was at St. Thomas University) or studying around our kitchen table in our small townhome. We were determined and certain that financial success would be ours if we just put in the time.

Play was also very important and somehow with this busy schedule, we were still able to fit in some very nice vacations for golf, skiing, tennis, and other activities. It was important for our relationship to not be all work and no play, and it still is. We also spent precious time at our parents' lake cabins (blessed that both families had one), where waterskiing, fishing, swimming, and cocktail hours were all part of the schedule. Life was good, as they say.

We always had a plan and tried not to leave anything to chance, and this was when we decided to plan our family. Jeanne had finished her MBA program, and I had another year to go. So, on the Sunday I graduated with my MBA degree, we announced to our parents that we were expecting our first child after almost five years of marriage. Perfect timing of course—just as we planned it. We were very fortunate to be blessed the way we were, and within the next five years, we had three beautiful children. The first was a boy, then a girl, followed by another boy. So, what do you do when you're at this point and in control? You decide that you should even up the sides and have a fourth child. Sure enough, it was a girl! Boy, girl, boy, girl. How could you plan any better? We were in control by the grace of God.

Financially, we were also doing very well. We both had great careers and had put together a plan before we were married and stuck with it. First, we only lived off my salary and saved

Jeanne's. Second, we had no credit card debt and no car loans. With the exception of our mortgage, we lived debt-free. I'm not sure that we were normal at that time, but it certainly felt like we had it together and had stuck to the itinerary. If you're familiar at all with Dave Ramsey's Financial Peace plan, you might say that we were early adopters of this, even before he published it. We just knew that financial freedom was important, and we were willing to sacrifice to get it. Because we were savers, we were also investors. We had modest stock portfolios and invested in many things, including real estate limited partnerships. We were having success and growing quite a nice nest egg. This saving habit of ours also allowed us to move up to a four-bedroom home as our family grew. It was a great life, and everything was progressing exactly as we envisioned. We were enjoying what we thought a normal life was supposed to look like and believed would always be there. What could possibly go wrong?

As I alluded to earlier, Jeanne and I had a very strong Christian faith. Mine was a Catholic tradition and hers was a Protestant one. God was very much a part of our life, starting with our wedding ceremony that was planned by us and officiated by both of our pastors. We attended church all the time, and when the children came, we were the family in the front of church, worshipping with our kids—or at least trying to keep them quiet while the rest of the church worshipped. Looking back at this time, I would have to say that my faith was more of a "head" faith and not much of a "heart" faith. I had attended six years of seminary from high school through college, and I knew the Bible. I had studied theology and felt very comfortable and informed. I have a very judicious viewpoint of life, and I could rationalize that I was living the way God wanted me to just by being successful. It makes sense, right? I give God a good hour of my life on Sundays, maybe some intermittent time during the week for prayer and scripture reading, and then I took over from there. He gave me certain abilities and I felt he wanted me to use them. It wasn't like we weren't generous. We always gave liberally to our church and other worthy charities we believed in. At the time, I believed this generosity made things right with God. After all, I did understand the concept that God blesses those who help others, and I've always tried to live my life by the Golden Rule.

Looking back, I am amazed at how I looked at life. I believed I had it all figured out. Have a good job, work hard, save, raise a loving family, go to church, help others as you're able, and life takes care of itself. There was no reason for not living the great American dream as Jeanne and I were. Life was good, normal, and we were in control of our future. Just the way it should be—a textbook description of how it's supposed to be done. We had thought of everything, right?

CHAPTER 2:

Family Business Time

As I mentioned, once we started having children, we realized that our two-bedroom townhome wasn't going to cut it any longer. So, we moved into a brand new four-bedroom home in the western suburbs of Minneapolis, which would allow for a more convenient commute for both of us. It would also provide us with plenty of room for family growth and expansion. The home was in a beautiful, new development with great neighbors all around us, and we were going to love it there! Our normal life would continue according to plan.

However, within a year of moving into our new home, my father called to talk business with me. He had started a very successful construction company in 1967 out of our family home in New Richmond, Wisconsin, and now, after twenty years, he was thinking of succession planning. His plan had always been for his boys to take over—keeping the business in the family as it continued growing. At that time, two of my three brothers and one other gentleman were working with him. Of course, Mom was always at his side, doing the books and running the design center for the custom home clients. His call to me was unexpected, and in a very direct manner he informed me he wanted to start selling the company in a couple of years. The substance of that conversation was that if I had any interest in being one of the owners, now was the time to say so! He didn't really seem concerned that we had just settled into our new home well over an hour away from New Richmond. For us, it just wasn't very good timing. How was this all going to fit into our plans? I had previously informed my dad, about a dozen years earlier (as I was graduating from college), that I needed to strike out on my own, and working for the family business just wasn't in the cards. I seemed to fit the mold of a lot of eldest sons. I just wanted my independence and the ability to make my own choices going forward.

I was doing very well at the time. I was a senior project manager for a commercial contractor in the Twin Cities and was involved with very high-profile clients. I would most definitely miss engaging with these individuals and the prestige of working on those projects if I were to leave. I saw a great future ahead of me, although ownership was probably *not* in the immediate future. I didn't really view the size and type of projects in western Wisconsin as all that appealing or glamorous. Even though New Richmond was considered part of the greater metro area, it was much more of a rural-type market. Jeanne and I really liked where we were living. We'd made numerous friends and were very unsure of moving so soon after settling into our new neighborhood.

To help with my decision, I asked the owner of a large concrete and masonry subcontractor that worked with our company to meet me for breakfast. I wanted to discuss the decision with him and get his thoughts. Mike was probably about twenty-five years my senior and a great businessman, and we had a very good relationship. I respected his honesty and straightforward talk. In other words, you always knew what he was thinking. Over breakfast at a popular restaurant, I explained to him the opportunity I was contemplating, and at some point, he stopped me and asked what my concern was.

I had three.

The first was that Derrick Construction was mostly known as a very good residential custom home builder—although the firm had done many commercial projects when the opportunities presented themselves. This was of concern to me because I did not have a strong interest in building residential houses. My experience and knowledge were in commercial/industrial projects. My second concern was that the market size was much smaller, and my final concern was about uprooting our family. Jeanne was very successful in large computer and software sales and her company's office was in downtown Minneapolis. Moving all the way to Wisconsin was probably not going to be an option. Of course, there was a chance I was just trying to come up with enough excuses to remain comfortable and stay where I was. Mike understood what was going on. He said, "Tell you what, Bill. Let's get up and walk around the restaurant and take a poll. We'll ask people what route they'd take—be a co-owner of their dad's family business versus remaining where they were and working for someone else." Mike certainly made his point, and this helped me realize that I was at that proverbial "fork in the road." It was time to make life happen and not just let it happen.

So, in early October 1988, I started working at the family construction company, Derrick Construction. It was my father, two brothers (Tom and Ron), myself, and Mike, who started working for my dad after graduating from college. Mike was married to our first cousin and my parents were her godparents. So, our business really was a family affair, with Mom overseeing the bookkeeping and interior design center. Our company was blessed with many skilled and loyal construction workers and was known for it its top-quality work throughout the entire St. Croix Valley area. The culture was one of working hard and doing what you were paid to do while making sure the client was happy.

Derrick was my fourth company to work for. As is always the case when starting a new job, there's going to be a difference between expectations and reality. That didn't take long to happen. Prior to agreeing with my father to come aboard, I thought that it was clear that my responsibilities included expanding and building up the commercial side of the business. On the very first day, Dad came into my office with a set of house plans and laid them on my desk. I inquired about the purpose of doing that, and he said he wanted me to do an estimate for the cost of the house. I objected and reminded him that I was here to develop our commercial business, not the residential. He asked if I had any commercial projects yet, and I reminded him that I had just started! He said, "Good. Then you'll have time to do what I asked." That was the first, but certainly not the last, business disagreement I had with my father. Perhaps it was a father versus oldest son thing. Maybe it had something to do with my desire to be in total control of my life and success. There is family and there is business, but my first lesson was that a family business can be different, and sometimes very challenging.

Within a couple of years, the four of us were preparing to buy out most of my parents' ownership in the company. Because the company now had to handle the livelihoods of four families versus only one, we realized that the firm had to grow. When my dad set up the succession plans, he made it clear he wanted us to work together and have "equal" say in making decisions. I always thought it was easy for someone to tell a team to work together when he never really had to do it himself. Many times, we ended up in a situation where all four of us were in charge, which really meant no one was in charge. In other words, "Too many chefs in the kitchen." We had a family business where ownership and management were the same, which I'm sure isn't too unusual. But sometimes it was difficult to make major decisions as it truly was a committee in charge of day-to-day operations. As president of the company, I never really felt I could make any decisions of consequence without getting the committee to agree. I also came to realize that my perspective about business was often different from my partners'—perhaps because of my business degree and that I was the only one with outside business experience. I saw things that I would like to change, but getting approval was always difficult unless it was something benign.

Of course, none of this stopped our desire to succeed. What seemed to work best for us was dividing the company into silos of business units. I managed the commercial business, Ron managed and expanded our Minnesota homebuilding business, Mike managed our Wisconsin homebuilding business, and Tom took care of managing our field operations. It worked very well. In fact, by the late 1990s, our company had revenue almost ten times more than what it was when we took over! I always thought we were proof you didn't always have to do things by the book to be successful. We had a couple of things going our way. Our county was, and still is, one of the fastest-growing counties in Wisconsin, as it is heavily influenced by the growth of Minneapolis/St. Paul. Second, like our parents, we had a very strong work ethic and weren't afraid to put in the extra time to succeed. We felt we could overcome any obstacle that might present itself with hard work and determination! We had grit!

Other things that helped us were great banking relationships, very good business advisors (both legal and financial), and the knack for knowing when to take a risk and when not to.

We had great subcontractors and vendors who were loyal to us because we treated them right, and they were able to grow with the firm. Finally, we were blessed to have our father around with his many years of experience in construction and land development. Yes, there were times of frustration, especially when he'd drop the familiar "if I were still running things around here" cliché. But as a family, we got through it. Jeanne always said what made us great was that we could argue during the workday then put it all behind us and come together as a family on the weekend.

The '90s were good for us, both business-wise and personally. With the move to the family business, we had to build a new house, and we settled into a young and growing suburb on the east side of the Twin Cities. This would conveniently allow for my commute to western Wisconsin and Jeanne's commute to Minneapolis. Daycare was convenient for us to share the load, and shortly after moving to our new home, we filled it up with another boy and girl! As I mentioned earlier, the perfect boy, girl, boy, girl combination.

After our third child was born, Jeanne and I made a very big decision. At a time when more and more women were entering the workforce, Jeanne decided to start a home-based business and at the same time be a stay-at-home mother, knowing our children would benefit from that. It was extremely tough for her to make this decision. She had become well respected and very successful in the computer software market. In fact, for many years her income was larger than mine, and for the most part we were still banking most of it. It certainly wasn't a pride thing for me to have a wife who outearned me, we were just very blessed to be in that position. But now Jeanne was putting her excellent sales and business skills to work as she grew her business, all while raising our four children. It was really wonderful for me to have Jeanne at home. We'd have great family dinners at night that would bring us together and strengthen our family ties. God had blessed us greatly, and we were very appreciative.

At the same time Jeanne left the workforce, we decided to cash in some investments and use our savings to pay off the mortgage. Not even forty years old yet and we were already mortgage-free! It was definitely the great American dream that many strive to attain by the time they retire. Of course, retirement wasn't even a thought yet, as we were just getting started. Jeanne and I were a great team, and we had the family, the home, and the finances to show for it.

Oh, did I mention we were in total control of our perfectly normal life, which was going seemingly according to plan?

CHAPTER 3:

The Calm Before the Storm

At the turn of the century, we were really rolling! Our construction business was growing and our "Derrick Built" brand was well-known in our market area. We were building beautiful "move-up" and higher-end custom homes, as well as many prominent, local commercial buildings. Many developers wanted us as a homebuilder in their developments. It was not unusual for us to build a beautiful home for a client one year and then build or expand their business a few years later—or vice versa. It was definitely a winning business model!

We were also very well-known as land developers in the St. Croix Valley area. As the area experienced rapid growth, our business continued to grow, and we had some of the best locations around. We took pride in our work—our homes were in great demand, and we did our developments right, without cutting corners. We used the excess profits from our construction operations to help fund and build the development side of our business. Our primary bank put together a consortium of banks to allow us the lending limit we needed to aggressively acquire and develop beautiful residential communities. Dad was also willing to lend a great deal of his cash to help fund the down payments that were necessary for our projects. This was a win-win situation. We paid him a larger interest rate than he could get at the bank, and in return, we had another source of cash to help us acquire more land. As an equal partner, Dad knew what we were investing in and knew the risk. At least I believed he knew the risk. As time went on, I became concerned about the amount of money we were borrowing from him, even though it was easier to get funds that way as opposed to going to a bank. We seemed to be confusing the fine line between partner and lender, yet he insisted time and time again that we look to his funds for buying land first. Because of this arrangement, we didn't need to use much of our own cash for land acquisition. Most of the time, we borrowed our down payment from Dad and the remaining funds from our banking consortium. This way we were able to use our available cash for the costs of development, such as grading streets and utilities. For this, we would "borrow" money from our construction companies with the understanding that it would be paid back after we started selling the lots. I mean, What could go wrong? We were in one of the fastest-growing counties in Wisconsin and were considered part of the growing metropolitan area of St. Paul and Minneapolis. Recessions never seemed to hit our area very hard, and with our diversified construction operations, we would just grow through any downturn.

Still, though, creating beautiful communities out of a raw piece of land is expensive and requires a lot of cash flow. So, what we'd do is distribute enough money from our construction operations profits to pay our income taxes, and the rest we'd just reinvest into land and development. With essentially five equal partners, it was difficult to object to our methodology, and why would you? We were on a big-time roll, believing there was only one way to go, and that was up.

During this time, we also were developing and leasing commercial buildings, teaming up with landowners, developers, and real estate brokers to create additional cash flow for our portfolio. Finally, we ventured into buying rural acreage for industrial development. We started by buying one hundred acres adjacent to a rail that we were going to develop into an industrial rail park. We bought another three hundred acres of farmland in the same community near the I94 freeway coming out of the Twin Cities. We believed this area was primed for robust industrial and commercial development.

Community-wise, we were all active in construction associations/organizations and were leaders in each one we were involved in. Many of us were also involved in neighborhood organizations and would volunteer when needed. We received numerous awards for our custom homes and commercial projects. We were recognized by the community as being partners and an asset to all who lived there.

Meanwhile, Jeanne and I were busy raising our family of six and keeping everything in order. Actually, Jeanne kept everything in order, and I tried to be present as needed. With four children we always had something going on with school activities, sports, and scouting. We enjoyed staying busy and found it very fulfilling.

We were also very involved with our church, and you would find our family there every Sunday. Jeanne was also very involved in Bible Study Fellowship (BSF) and eventually convinced me to participate in an evening men's BSF. Because of that, I was able to take my children with me weekly to participate in the children's program while I participated in the adult men's program. As a family, we were reading the Bible and learning how God has worked in the lives of others since the beginning of time and how important it is to have a personal relationship with him. Personally, I was no stranger to the Bible. I had spent fourteen years in parochial schools as part of my upbringing, and therefore I always brought a nicely marked up Bible to the BSF evening classes. I realized that with all the time spent on building our business, I had gotten away from studying God's Word regularly. So the seven years in BSF really helped me and enabled me to see how God was working in my life once again.

My faith was starting to become a more integral part of my life, and I had no way of knowing how important that would be later.

In 2006, I was sitting in church one Sunday listening to a guest pastor give the sermon. His message was that everyone will experience storms in their lives—some are going into one, some are in the midst of one, and some are coming out of one. He based his message on Luke 6:48, which says, "They [those who hear Christ's words and put them into action] are like a man building a house, who dug down deep and laid the foundation on rock. When a flood came, the torrent struck that house but could not shake it, because it was well built."

Vince Miller, who gave that sermon, and years later would become a good friend and mentor, is a wonderful speaker and has a special way of delivering God's Word in a meaningful manner. I listened intently that day to his message—a reminder that some of us will have to go through the storms of life. The message was clear: we better have our beliefs and convictions based on a solid foundation (God's Word) to get through life's storms without being washed away. Certainly, as a builder, I could appreciate the necessity of a solid foundation. As a Christian with a strong belief in God, I felt I had the right foundation—didn't I? Besides, I had everything figured out and had no fear of going through a storm. I had a great family, a nice house in the suburbs, a cabin on a lake in northwest Wisconsin, and a very successful business to support my acquired lifestyle. Great sermon, Vince, but thankfully it didn't apply to me! No storm here (so I thought)!

Our business continued to seemingly fire on all cylinders. We continued to accrue land for development in 2005 and 2006, easily getting the bank debt we needed to secure it. Our residential and commercial construction companies were doing very well and exceeding expectations. Our businesses had lots of money in the bank, and our hard work and long hours continued to pay off.

However, something wasn't right. Somewhere inside me there was what I would describe as *discontent*. I had become driven by the size of my personal financial statement, and I looked forward to updating it every year just to see how much it had grown. I was losing track of what was important, and Jeanne was constantly reminding me that she married me for who I was, not for my money. Looking back, I can see that despite our family business' success, I wasn't entirely happy about where I was. When asked, most of us would say our top three priorities should be God, family, and business. However, it seemed like at this particular time, in spite of the success—or maybe because of the success—my top three priorities seemed to be business, more business, and tied for third, God and family.

I believe I was experiencing what many would call the "curse of success." It's easy to get knocked off track during extended periods of prosperity, and that's exactly what was happening. I was becoming very self-sufficient, and I depended on my own inner strength, grit, and creativity to succeed. I believed that I could do no wrong and that our business was indestructible. Think about it, business is so easy. You find a product or service others want, you charge more than it costs to produce it, and you collect the money and put it in the bank. This is the complicated stuff that I learned in MBA School. (No sarcasm there!)

I was also developing what I believed was an unhealthy attitude of pride. Not the type of pride where you're proud of what you do or who you are, but the pride of being always in control, being able to fix any problem, and having the solution to any challenge. It was basically a lack of trusting in God. I mean, Why would you need to depend on God if you're thinking success was a result of your own actions? As a leader and business owner, one's thought process dictates that we need to be the ultimate problem solver, one who can overcome all obstacles. However, we must be able to exercise humility and admit that we're not all-knowing. It's imperative to realize the importance of spiritual guidance and direction that only the Creator can empower us with.

Good stuff, huh?

I wish that either I would have realized this on my own or someone would have shared it with me earlier so I didn't have to learn the hard way. The reality though is that God works in a mysterious manner, and he has his reasons.

In the meantime, we were flying high with lots of financial success. It seemed like everything we did was successful. Life was good, and up to this point, I was still in control.

CHAPTER 4:

Didn't See That Coming!

I n the period from 2004 to 2007, we had a lot going on with our business. Most of it, if not all of it, was very good. We were still acquiring land, the necessary financing, and continuing plans to develop more finished residential/commercial lots to add to our inventory. One of the new residential neighborhoods we added was a 166-acre parcel that consisted of six phases of clustered housing. We had developed phase one and were well into building and selling the upscale homes planned in this bedroom community. It was a community in the East Metro area near the scenic St. Croix River, a very desirable part of town. Across the river in western Wisconsin, all our developments were firing on all cylinders as well. It was build, build, build!

Thus, both our residential and commercial construction operations continued strongly, which enabled us to feed our development operations. This allowed us to make the required interest payments and meet the necessary expenses to develop our properties. The years 2004, 2005, and 2006 were high-water marks for revenue and profitability. But even as construction revenue and profit dipped in 2007, we weren't overly concerned, because we were still doing well and expectations for continued growth were strong. Again, we were in the right place, as St. Croix County has consistently been one of the fastest-growing counties in Wisconsin. In addition to this, the migration to the east from the Twin Cities continued. More and more people were willing to commute from western Wisconsin as land, lot prices, and housing costs were less expensive than in the immediate Twin Cities. Developers flocked to western Wisconsin to buy and develop farmland that was relatively inexpensive compared to prices in the suburbs. Certainly, we were concerned with the amount of competition for land that was driving up prices and starting to contribute to the potential of overbuilding. However, we took pride in having the more desirable neighborhoods in the more desirable locations. Remember, the key to real estate is "location, location, location!" We believed that despite the increased competition and the slight downturn we were experiencing in 2007, success would continue for quite some time.

To take advantage of the prosperity that we had built during this time, and to find a way to buy out our father's remaining shares, we used an Employee Stock Ownership Plan (ESOP) to accomplish this. The plan was for the ESOP to buy out our parents' remaining ownership plus a portion of our ownership to allow the employees to own 30 percent of the company. We would still maintain control, but this would allow our employees to directly share in the profits. This was no simple task to accomplish. Much of my time was spent working with accountants, attorneys, banks, and appraisers to properly prepare the documentation to meet the Department of Labor's approval. We expected to close on July 1, 2007, but at the last minute, the bank that was going to finance the purchase for the ESOP decided to pull out. They said it was because of the potential slowdown in our industry. Of course, we didn't see it that way. So as an alternative to bank financing, we each decided to personally loan the funds for the shares we were selling as a note to the ESOP. That seemed simple enough. Once the appraiser determined the current value of the company and we agreed to the price and who the ESOP's trustee was going to be, we were ready to close. On October 1, 2007, we became an "Employee Owned" company and the employees now owned 30 percent of the business. The ESOP would pay for the shares they purchased with its share of the profits each year. Easy, right? As long as we remained profitable, which should be no problem given our track record.

On January 2, 2008, we were surprised when it was announced that our bank, S&C Bank, based in New Richmond, had been acquired by Anchor Bank, located in Madison, Wisconsin. Anchor Bank was doing this to take advantage of the growing market in northwestern Wisconsin. Most of our real estate and development loans were with S&C Bank and the other banks that were in the consortium that S&C put together to serve our borrowing needs. S&C was owned locally, and our company had had a business relationship with S&C and its predecessor (Bank of New Richmond) almost from the start of our firm in 1967. They were also an excellent client of ours, as we had built most of their banking facilities in the St. Croix Valley, including their flagship bank in New Richmond. This was a strong and meaningful relationship that was being changed without warning. To soften the blow, representatives of Anchor Bank came to our office that same day to assure us very little would change. Of course they were going to say that. They boldly stated that because of their large portfolio of loans with developers in southern Wisconsin, they could help teach us how to be more successful with land development. Somewhat of an arrogant comment, wouldn't you say?—one they would regret in the not-too-distant future. One positive in this was that our banking relationship would remain with the same person we had been dealing with as he decided to stay following the buyout.

After the announcement we were approached by many other banks who were interested in our business and were curious to know if we were going to keep our relationship with this larger regional bank. Although there was some discomfort in this change, we did see the additional banking strength that Anchor brought to the table, and we decided to ride it out for a while.

However, it felt good to be wanted by so many other banks. We had become an important business to the banking industry with all our real estate holdings. It felt good, and we were in control.

Meanwhile, something else was happening that was going to have a much greater effect on our business. I believe it started with the price of gas going beyond $3.00 per gallon on its way to $4.00 in 2008. This made the cost of commuting from western Wisconsin to the Twin Cities much more expensive. Along with that, land costs had escalated to a point where it was hard to find land that made sense to develop. The financial incentive to move to the St. Croix Valley wasn't as great as it had been earlier in the decade. Now there was talk of a recession (which actually started in December of 2007). Nationally, a downturn in the housing market was being predicted, but most expected a decrease of no more than 10 percent and only lasting for six months to a year. With the cash reserves that we had, we felt we would have no problem "riding it out."

Well into 2008, it became apparent that the housing market was collapsing. What made this different for us is that we were rarely hit hard by a recession. This is because our location has always maintained a resilient and strong economy. Not this time, however. We were really feeling this one. Our 2007 revenue was almost 30 percent less than in 2006. In 2008, we were down another 27 percent. Our revenue was now only about half of our revenue from two years earlier. We could barely cover our overhead at this point and eked out a very small profit in 2008. We didn't want to cut costs and employees too quickly, because we were holding on to the hope that this was going to be a brief downturn. We wanted to make sure that we kept our employees in place for the recovery that was sure to follow. As I mentioned earlier, we had a very healthy cash reserve, and we were using it to feed the monster we had created with the real estate and development side of our business. As the recession continued to drag out through 2008, we started to be concerned about what would happen if we "ran out of money." We certainly didn't see that happening to us, but with talk of the subprime mortgage collapse and the housing bubble burst, there was certainly some concern. Later that year, we met with the president of our bank to get an update when he and his team were up from Madison. Rumors were already floating around that the debt that they took on to buy out S&C Bank was a burden. They assured us that they were strong and would weather this downturn. We then ask what we should do if we were to use up all our available cash and line of credit to handle our debt obligations. Their response was one we couldn't believe: "Borrow more money."

After distributing enough money to allow for the ESOP to pay for their required stock payments, paying our interest and debt obligations, and earning a small profit in 2008, we were quickly running low on cash, the lifeblood of any small business. All the treasure that we had built up since 1990 was eroding away. Our industry and our business were in the bull's-eye of what would be called the "Great Recession." It was the worst time for the real estate industry since the 1930s, when the Great Depression separated many companies from their real estate holdings because of bankruptcies. Our business was falling off a cliff. Much of our real estate was now worth only 25 percent of its previous value. It really didn't matter what it was worth though because no one was buying it anyway. I hadn't bargained for this. This wasn't in my plan for my life. I had thought that with the success we were having, I might look at some sort of partial retirement when I reached my mid to late fifties. That plan was not going to happen.

I thought about that Vince Miller sermon in 2006 about the storms in life. I realized that his message was very prophetic. The storm that I had denied would ever happen was here. It was time to question whether I really had the foundation to survive the storm. I was starting the questioning process that I suspect most of us go through when the storms of life come. I quickly realized that the foundation was not all the wealth we had accumulated, because that was going quickly. The foundation I needed was a deeper and more meaningful faith in God, and it was time that I seriously turn back to him for the help that I would need. For me, that meant starting to be more prayerful and consistently reading his Word in the Bible. I would assume that many God-fearing people going through a financial crisis naturally begin by opening the book of Job when looking for answers in the Bible. Job was a man of God who trusted in him for all things and was truly blessed with riches, wealth, and family. God allowed Satan to tempt Job by taking all that away, but Job remained steadfast to God. Much of the book describes Job's searching for the reason with his friends who come to visit. Job was steadfast in his trust in God and in Job 42:2, he declares, "I know that you can do all things; no purpose of yours can be thwarted." In the end, God restored his fortunes, but it's not about that so much as it is about Job realizing that his life is only about God, whether he is rich or poor.

I liked it better when business was good—when I was in control. Somehow, I was starting to think that maybe I didn't have as much control over my success as I'd thought. I didn't like that feeling and wanted to fight to regain control over the life I was used to. I was also starting to struggle with how I felt about being part of a family business. Five partners wanting different things from the business. Five partners with different thoughts on how business should be done. It was hard to lead a business in five different directions, although we had done a very good job and had had a very good run of success to this point. I boasted that we were proof that you don't have to run a business by the book to be successful. I guess I might have spoken too soon. However, we had more important things to think about now—namely, how our business was going to survive this recession. We went from the pinnacle of success to having the rug pulled out from under us. A very different journey was about to happen. One that I wasn't prepared for, nor one that I wanted.

I was no longer in control!

CHAPTER 5:

The Journey Through the Storm

F ive years is a long time, especially when it delays what you believed were the latter years of your career. When this storm started, there was no way that we thought it would last that long. But the residential construction and development industry was the bull's-eye of this recession. Even though the recession officially ended in 2009, the carryover continued in our industry straight through to 2012. Remember that this recession came on with a bang. However, most thought it would be over in about a year after a 10 percent downturn or so. So much for the experts. I believe there was only one economist that I know of who predicted the depth, breadth, and severity of this recession in our industry. It was a debilitating disaster for many in our line of work. I quickly realized that I was going through a major life storm, one that was much more severe than anything I had ever thought possible.

This storm caused me to pause and think about what was important. I realized that my priorities in life needed to be reordered to where they should have been. My first priority needed to be God; second, my family; and third, business and others. I had been so fixed on business and financial success as well as personal recognition during the past years that I had pushed God and my family to the side. I'd certainly become one of those who say, "Someday when I have enough money, I will . . ." (fill in the blank). This storm was God's way of telling me that I was off course, and he was calling me to change my ways. But I had a business that needed all my attention, and the problems were consuming me. What do I do? Perhaps it was time to wake up my Lord in the boat and ask him to calm the seas! I realized that this was the time for me to concentrate on God's word and to really start praying.

Looking back on this time, I can see that God placed events and people in my life to help me through the troubles that always seemed to lay ahead. These "ordinary" people and events delivered powerful messages that helped propel me forward and gave me hope that we would survive the carnage that lay all around us.

The problem for us during this time, simply put, was too much debt and not enough money to service it. We depended on the profitability of our construction companies to pay the holding costs of the land we purchased and stockpiled for future development. With the residential business losing money and the commercial business barely breaking even, we continued to use up cash on hand. Of course, the size of our business had constricted. Where once we had almost one hundred employees, we were now down to about forty. That was very hard as a family business. We knew that many families depended on us and now they were feeling the tough times of this recession. It was very difficult to let good people go. We hung on as long as we could, but eventually we made some very difficult layoffs. At our high-water mark, we had over $40 million in construction sales and at our low point during this time we barely accomplished $10 million. Margins were low and it was very difficult, if not impossible, to cover overhead. Dad would come into my office quite frequently, and one time he explained how this recession was different from any other that he had ever experienced. He explained that as a home builder, if you built ten homes in a typical year, you might only build seven or eight during a normal recession. But with this recession, you were lucky to build two or three a year. Very hard to survive with those numbers. He always said that putting your money in real estate is a great investment because it doesn't go down in price. However, even he was shaking his head now as much of our real estate holdings were appraised at 25 percent of what we'd paid. Buying and holding land for future development was not working for us at this time, and it was becoming increasingly difficult to even pay the interest on our bank debt.

It seemed like it was the new reset, and we were on the losing end of this reset!

To add to the stress, Dad's visits became more and more about how his debt was going to be paid. He too had not planned on this when he loaned the money to our real estate partnerships, of which he was a part. The concern that I'd had was now coming home to roost. His visits to my office became harder and harder as more times than not they were about how his debt would be paid. And this lasted well past the end of the recession. It was difficult to tell my dad that he would have to wait until we got the banks squared away. I'm sure that it was frustrating to hear that, but I didn't know what else to say. I promised him that somehow, someway, he and Mom would be paid back. As someone who always felt free to speak what was on his mind, he felt free to let me know how we were messing with his money, which was difficult to hear. Not only was this humbling, but this was also maddening. I was trying to stand in a storm that kept blowing stronger and from many directions. It hurt that we were causing my dad and mom to question our ability to cover our debt with them. It seemed to me that this time caused my dad to question our leadership and whether our company would truly be the company he thought it should be. We were doing our best to lead our family business through this terrible time, but it was very frustrating that I felt Dad was disappointed in us. All I could do was ask for patience. I loved and respected my dad very much and there was no way that I wanted him to be disappointed in me. Sometimes it is very tough to be involved in a family business, especially during hard times.

In early 2009, I was meeting with my peer group of contractors and explained, based on the information I had received, that the recession was going to end later in 2009 (which technically it did). One of the members of the group and a close friend of mine quickly responded by stating that for us in the real estate and construction industry, this will be our Great *Depression*. We had better be prepared for the worst regardless of when it ended. There was just too much overbuilding and too much land to be absorbed any time soon. I was shocked and in denial of what he stated. I just didn't want to believe it. I believe that I was still processing what was happening to me and our company. Regardless, I was determined to stay optimistic while realizing we had a lot of work to do to get through this time as we struggled to make ends meet.

I was questioning my naivety that a crisis of this nature could hit my life. As I looked back, I saw that it was foolish of me to think that I could be isolated from the type of crisis that many business owners experience. I was blindsided and yet, at the same time, I realized that my partners and I had to take the necessary steps to dig out of this crisis. But we didn't have a playbook or a checklist to do this. I started questioning if I had the necessary business experience and knowledge to lead us through. I was certainly feeling humbled by this whole thing. However, I realized that feeling sorry for myself was not going to get the job done. It was time to muster up all my God-given talents and use them at each fork in the road that we came to. At this point, I began asking God for forgiveness for my foolish and prideful attitude. I was learning a valuable lesson and began asking God for deliverance from this crisis. I was ready for this to end and was ready for God to deliver a Job-like ending for me and our business.

Midway through 2009, after reviewing our cash situation with our controller, it appeared that there was a good chance we would run out of cash to pay our interest costs if we didn't ask for some sort of "workout" with the financial institutions that held our debt. Many other builders and developers had already started that process, but because of our strong financial situation, we were able to hold off much longer. It was very difficult to admit that we would ever be in a situation where we couldn't meet our financial obligations. However, as the recession lingered on, it became obvious to me that we needed to start the process and I proposed this to my partners. It was understandable that they wanted to wait things out a little while longer, but I stood strongly on this, and we agreed it was time to hire our real estate attorney to start working on a plan with our lenders. Little did we know what we were in for. We had always paid our debts on schedule and never asked for any help. Surely our lenders would understand the situation we were in and would willingly help us out. After all, they were more than willing to lend us the money and consider us "partners." We saw this as a temporary thing that would pass in a couple of years. We just needed help to bridge the gap.

Late in 2009, with the help of our attorney, we submitted a proposal to each of our lenders that asked for lower interest rates and deferments on both interest and principal payments. We stressed how this was important to stave off foreclosure on our real estate. That would be disastrous because if one bank foreclosed on us, then they all would, and they would be left fighting over our assets. We stressed that with help during this extremely hard time, we could recover and make full payment down the road.

We were surprised by the initial nonchalant attitude that met the proposals. The answer was generally "No," or "Not right now," or "Let's wait and see what it is like when these loans come up for renewal." Our attorney advised us that they would put off negotiating with us if we continued to make payments and advised us to stop making payments to get their attention. This was a hard moment for us because we took pride in always taking care of our obligations. Based on the advice of our attorney, though, we decided to stop making payments. Besides, who were we kidding? We were going to run out of cash very soon anyway. We stopped making payments and, yes, that got their attention. In addition to this, on a hunch that our major line of credit would not be renewed, we instructed our controller to borrow all but a couple thousand dollars from the line and deposit the funds in a bank with whom we did not have any loans. I was trying to find as much "dry powder" as possible to get us through this time. We needed to build the garrison as best we could and the sandbags to do this with was cash.

Now we were negotiating. It was not fun, but we were negotiating. It was as if our relationship turned into a poker game,
for real! Certainly, it wasn't pleasant when one of the bankers
held up our personal guarantees and threatened to collect on
those if we didn't keep our loans current. We were starting to
realize the seriousness of those personal guarantees we were
required to sign to borrow money. Another banker questioned
why they should give a deal to a bunch of wealthy businessmen.
We had to remind him that we may be asset-rich but in fact were
now cash-poor. There was the constant threat of foreclosure
as we continued to work our way through this. We repeatedly
reminded our lenders that we were good for the debt in the long
run. I hate to put it this way, but we had to convince them that
we were better alive than dead. This time was no picnic for the
banking industry either, and many banks (approximately four
hundred between 2009–2011) were failing and being forced
to shut down or being sold to other banks. The cause of their
failures was directly attributed to bad real estate loans. The
stress became worse and worse and sometimes almost unbear-
able. Each of us bore the stress differently, but I felt that it was
important to try to put on as good an attitude as possible to the
employees, even though we were dealing with survival. They
needed to know that we were going to get through this and not
jump ship. Proverbs 22:7 (NLT) says that "the borrower is servant to the lender." Wow was that ever jumping off the page
of my Bible. We were living it. It seemed like I was constantly
negotiating with bankers, trying to work out an arrangement

that would allow them to get paid but also decrease the amount of cash going out of our accounts.

As if there weren't enough financial issues to deal with, it was time for the ESOP to make its next annual payment. To do this we would need to distribute enough money to the ESOP, and, in turn, it would make its next payment to my parents and the rest of us. We didn't have the cash available to do this, but even if we did, we knew it would not look well with our lenders if we essentially took money out of the firm to pay the owners. After contacting Jim, who was the principal of our accounting firm, and explaining the situation, he immediately confirmed that we couldn't and shouldn't make the payment. After meeting with him and our ESOP attorney, it was decided that our only choice was to suspend and terminate our ESOP and wind it down over the next few months. But first I needed to fly to Florida and meet with my parents to explain the situation to them, to tell them that they would be getting their shares back because we couldn't afford to pay them, particularly not at a time when we were losing money. They were very understanding, especially after I showed them our current financial status. I still believe that it was a great idea for us to do the ESOP but not, unfortunately, in the worst economic downturn in the last eighty years! The fact that we tried to make it work paid dividends with our employees, as they were very appreciative that we tried to sell them part of the company.

As I said, we were in survival mode. In 2 Samuel, chapter 24, the great King David takes a census of all his troops. At first, this seems to be a logical and innocent act by David, but because it was done with a dependence on the size of his troops and his kingdom, not his dependence on God, it was wrong. When reading and studying this, I asked why he would do such a thing after all God had done for him?

Suddenly, I was convicted by this point.

I was more dependent on the size of our bank account than I was dependent on God for survival. Certainly it was very important for us to know what we had and how we could make the payments we agreed to, but during this time of survival, I was being taught that God requires me to trust him. Proverbs 15:22 says, "Plans fail for lack of counsel, but with many advisers they succeed." It was time for me to seek out wise counsel. It was time for me to learn from others what I needed to learn and how to get through this. Now, my partners concentrated on operations, and I concentrated on our survival with our lenders. It was time for me to exercise humility and realize that I couldn't control everything. I was most definitely apprehensive, even very afraid, of what the future held. The unease was all-consuming, especially as I heard and saw the misery other developers were going through with their lenders.

Later one day during this time, Alan, who is our company's financial advisor for our retirement plan, stopped in my office. He was there that day helping our employees with their individual plans. Alan had also been my personal financial advisor for many years, and we knew each other quite well. Without an invitation, he sat down, looked around my office, and asked me what was going on. He said it looked like a bomb had gone off! Now, I was never known for keeping a clean and organized desk, but I must admit that the state of my office did not look good. I explained to him that nothing was going right: Our longtime controller had left for a better job, and her replacement left a short time later. I needed to find a replacement, the banks were not as cooperative as I thought they should be, and the construction business was not good.

I guess I thought he was there to join me for the pity party.

Alan was having none of it, though. He asked me one question: "What was the worst thing that could happen?" I gave him a puzzled look and asked what he meant by that. Without thinking further about where the question was going, I stated that our lenders could foreclose on us at any time, take our real estate, collect on our personal guarantees, and take many of our personal assets and bank accounts, leaving us with very little leftover. Since they didn't have a corporate guarantee on our construction companies, we would still have those, but we would have to start over at a smaller level. He suggested that now that I knew the "worst," go to work every day committed to improving upon that worst-case scenario. Stay positive with the attitude that you'd come out swinging every day and work diligently to improve the situation. I believe that Alan was trying to tell me to quit thinking about the worst and start thinking about the best that could happen. Great advice for whenever we are in or entering the unknown and are in risky territory. The timing of Alan's advice was perfect. I took that piece of advice to heart.

One of the first breaks we received during this time was when Ed, our banker at Anchor Bank, resigned and left the bank while we were trying to work out new loans with them. Ed was more than our banker; he was a friend who cared deeply for the Derrick family. He realized that our hearts were in the right place and was willing to help us in any way he could, but at the time, he could provide no assistance. It was out of his hands, as they say. About two weeks after he left Anchor Bank, I was able to find out which bank he was working for and called him to arrange a meeting. When I met with Ed, I asked him if he was ready to be our banker again, because we could sure use one right now! Ed was already putting a plan together, and using the few unleveraged assets that he knew we had, he helped us obtain a USDA-backed loan, which enabled us to pay back the line of credit that was now well overdue. It also gave us the additional funds we needed to help get through that troublesome period. This was the beginning of seeing the light at the end of the tunnel.

It was also during this time that the New Richmond school superintendent, Morrie, approached me about the possibility of negotiating an $8 million school remodel project. It was the last of several major construction projects that the school system was doing, and he wanted to see more local involvement in the projects. We worked hard to make sure we were able to convince the school board that we would finish on time and under budget.

We had one further hurdle and that was providing a bond for the project. Remember, we had used up all our commercial construction company's cash reserves funding commitments to our banks for our real estate holdings and our operating costs as we struggled to break even during this difficult time. Without this cash reserve, it was going to be difficult to obtain the necessary bond for the project. To complicate matters, we were in the process of switching bonding agents as requested by our bonding company. When I sat down with our new agent to review our pathetic financials, I begged for any way to get this bond. We had secured a very nice job for our company that would help us get through the year, but we needed that bond. Our agent also had a good relationship with our bonding company and quickly arranged for a meeting at our office. Dick, our longtime bonding company representative, flew up from Chicago to meet with us. I told our story of how we'd gotten to this point and what we were doing to not only survive but to get through this time. I leveraged our relationship with our longtime bonding company and explained how important this project was to our survival. Dick, who had handled our bonding for years, understood us, believed and trusted in us, and appreciated our loyalty over the years. He saw and understood the situation that we were in and was willing to bond this important project, provided we put a minimal amount of cash back into our company and left it there during the ten-month project. It was a very reasonable request, and the bond was issued to us. This was another example of learning to depend on others and the help they could provide while learning a lesson in humility.

We finished this large project on time (if not early) and within the school district's budget. After the project was completed, I met with Morrie once more to express our thanks for trusting us and our firm. This project was crucial to our survival, and I don't know what we would've done without it.

Mike is the general manager of one of the car dealerships in town, and a client as well. One day I was talking to Mike on the phone and telling him about our situation. I told him that the hardest part of what we were going through was that I didn't know when or how it was going to end. The apprehension level was high, and it would sure be nice to know how this unexpected crisis was going to end. He said that we could determine the ending now if we wanted to. I asked him how that was possible, and he said quit. I said that quitting was not an option, and he suggested that no matter what happens, I keep that in mind each day. He suggested that I read the book *Unbroken*, the true story of Louis Zamperini's survival during WWII. His story of survival against all odds was very inspirational to me.

There are a lot of moments in a financial storm like this one when you just don't know how much longer you can bear it. Don't quit, no matter what. How many times in life do we think we've failed at something when in fact all we did was quit? People do this all the time when they come to a hurdle that they think is a wall instead of finding a way through it or around it. There are a lot of moments in a financial storm when you just don't know how much longer you can bear it! But at the right time (God's timing), you get that email or that phone call from someone encouraging you to keep moving forward. God is there, he is always there. The question is, Do we trust in him enough to help us through the storm by his means and in his way? Trust in him and don't quit.

There were many others that I received wise counsel from during this crisis. We kept our relations cordial with our lenders, making sure they understood that our intent was good. There were times I would come home at night and shed tears, especially after days when all appeared to be lost. Those were the times I had to drop to my knees and pray for God's glory through it all. We kept going and were able to turn what looked like a hopeless situation into a hopeful one, and as our market started to turn for the better in the 2011–2012 period, we could see that survival was going to be possible.

My prayers were for survival during this storm and to heal us financially so that we could get through it. I can look back and see that God placed many people in our path who not only cared for us but helped us tremendously. I'm amazed at how blind I was before this storm about how God was working in my life. It took a financial crisis that almost broke us financially for my eyes to be open to his wonderful workings. Yes, I was quick to ask God to get us out of this storm, but I slowly realized that it was going to happen in God's time and not mine.

I can now see that God allows these storms in our lives for our own good and his glory. Many times, when bad things happen, people will ask, "Where's God?" He is there, right by our side, but it's a two-way street. My storm helped me to see this and caused me to draw closer to him by increasing my personal study and reading of his Word. I have read through the Bible several times since this happened, and each time, God's Word teaches me something new. That, as well as engaging in more intimate daily prayer, has improved my awareness of his presence, and I most certainly recognize his workings as I look for his guidance and trust in him.

And yet at this point, I was still asking the following question: "Did God have another reason or purpose for this storm in my life?"

CHAPTER 6:

My Response

I imagine that many who go through storms in their lives just want to be done with them and move on. Having gone through this uninvited time in my life, I believe that one must take time to reflect on what has just happened and what can be learned from it. I believe very strongly now that God's purpose in our life storms is for us to learn from them, become better, and for us to be drawn closer to him. But this is up to us. As I went through that time, I can see that God stripped away many things in my life that I thought were important. This in turn motivated me to once again seek him out through more time reading the Bible, prayer, and reflection. It's kind of funny how that works. When we are going through the good times in life, we seem to forget about God, but when life turns on its head, we turn to God and ask for his help. As previously mentioned, my prayers slowly changed from "Fix it, God" to being more reflective and trying to understand a purpose in the tough time we were experiencing. Why, God, were we going through this? What did he want me to learn from it, and what was the ultimate purpose for this? Here I was, the guy who'd been so sure of his purpose a few short years earlier, now questioning everything apparently. Humbled and certainly a little poorer, it didn't seem that I was the successful and educated business-person that I thought I was. I was being forced to depend on something other than myself to get through this.

There was still the question of what lay ahead, but all of this caused me to pause and think about what I believe are some important life lessons. When going through life's conflicts, we need to spend time in reflection to better understand the lessons and to reap the full "benefit" from what we just experienced.

My observations:

Life can be much simpler than we make it. What I mean is that with any small amount of success, we start to fill our lives with clutter and stuff that we think we must have. It might be a vacation home, fancier cars, grown-up toys, fancy vacations, etc. These are things that in themselves aren't bad, but when we become too possessive of them, they can become idols that become more important to us than our God who provides for us. By going through this storm, I realized the importance of letting go of the things that don't matter. We can start to worship these things, as if we must have them. But must we? We see these things as our treasures in life, but they really aren't our treasures; they are more like baggage that weighs us down and holds us back from seeing and understanding God's purpose for us. I believe that when things are stripped from our life, it helps lead us back to where we can trust in God for our future, not the things that we have. I see now that God didn't put me here to complicate life with more and more things, but rather to trust in him and to bless others with what he has blessed me with.

Gratitude. This time in my life taught me that I needed to be more grateful for the blessings God has given me. It's easy to take our blessings for granted until we start losing them. Don't wait for this to happen before being grateful. Let the harder times develop a grateful heart in you. Live each day with an attitude of gratitude! Consciously think of the blessings you are grateful for every day. Write them down. Then stop and thank God. The spirit of gratefulness and a joyful heart that you exhibit will also be a blessing to others and will help make their lives better. No matter where you are, you will find that if you have a grateful heart, it will be very hard to be anxious about what you don't have!

Humility. During this time, I became a humbler and more compassionate person toward others. I don't believe humility and compassion were void in my life before this, but I certainly realized that to be a better husband, friend, and leader, humility and compassion needed to be refined in my life. I believe that before this happened, I was more worried about myself than about what was happening to others. I had never gone through a difficult financial crisis before, so it was very difficult for me to understand those who were having either business or personal financial troubles. I was the type who expected others to pull their weight, as we all have our own hurts to navigate through life. I experienced the compassion that God blessed me with as he helped me cope and wisely venture through this time. Now he was asking me to show the same type of compassion to others during their times of hurt. I can better appreciate what others experience and this has made me a more relational person with others. I have learned that the time I take to stay in touch with others, through notes, phone calls, emails, and even texts, can make a huge difference in someone else's day. I believe this has made me a better leader, and I see compassion and humility as strengths that all effective leaders need. Now I take more time to listen to others and try to relate to them and understand where they're at. Very simply, I've learned that it isn't just about me!

Let go of control. I now understand that I am not as in control of all things in my life as I thought I was. I see that I only have control over those things that God allows me to have control over. God is in control of the rest, and I need to surrender to him and have faith. As a leader, I believe that this was my most valuable lesson but the toughest one to learn. As stated earlier, I believed that being in control of my destiny here in this world was most important, especially as a leader. I am not saying that you avoid doing the planning that needs to be done. I am not saying that you shouldn't depend on the God-given talents and skills that you have. But sometimes we need to let go and understand that, ultimately, it's God's purposes that we need to accomplish in our lives. I learned to be so much more dependent on him during this storm, as I realized so many things were beyond my control. Because of this valuable lesson, I feel that I'm free to strive to live each day for his purpose, without the concern of being in control of everything. Now I allow God to use me, my talents, and my skills for the purpose he is continually revealing to me.

Redefine success. My definition of success has changed as a result of this storm. I have come to realize that my success in life was no longer going to be measured by the size of my bank account. My financial status took a major hit during that time, which caused me to reconsider the importance of financial status and its purpose. I no longer view the numbers on spreadsheets as numbers to be maximized and controlled. Instead, now I count them as blessings that perhaps can be a blessing to others. When this storm was at its height, this was a very hard lesson for me—that I might not be in as much control of my financial well-being as I thought. I realized that my goal of financial freedom and retiring at sixty was going to be delayed. After much turmoil, I realized that I just had to give it all to God and that I was going to need to be happy no matter where he was taking me financially. My legacy was going to be determined by something other than the financial size of my estate. Even getting through this business malaise and starting on the road back to financial well-being, I was determined to not make money the most important thing in my life. What was more important now was learning what my purpose in this life really was. As a follower of Christ, I needed to come to grips with God's plan and just trust him going forward. I was learning that my purpose needed to align with God's purpose. It took this major business storm for me to start seeing this.

Finally, in 2011, after three-plus long years, both of our construction companies were once again profitable, although modestly compared to the hole that we had dug since the recession began in 2007. But we could use those profits as a start to help pay off our debt. In addition to this, our residential lot sales started to pick up, which also helped in lowering our debt. Unfortunately, we had to compete with low-priced lots that were now being liquidated by banks who had acquired them through foreclosures of developers who were unable to survive. This meant that some of our lot sales were unable to cover the debt owed against them, meaning that we had to put additional cash into those sales to obtain the release from our lender. It was another tough lesson, as we were losing money on some of the lots we were selling. Eventually though, we were able to refinance some of our loans, which strengthened our financial position. We were slowly digging our way out. It was important for us to stay true to our word that we would pay our debts and that the financial institutions would be rewarded for the trust they had placed in us. We were starting to acquire new banking partners who would help us transition back to a healthier business climate. It was now time for us to move from a time of survival to a time of thriving once again. The effects from the Great Recession would be felt for a few more years as we worked hard to get rid of the large debt chained around our ankles. There were plenty of bargains for land and lots during this time, but we were a seller not a buyer. I was okay with this because I believed God was pointing us in a new and healthier direction. There were still going to be bumps in the road, but I had confidence and trust in his way going forward.

I learned a lot about working through business debt during that time. I could recite a bunch of banking terms we learned, but that really isn't what is important. I was told by more than one banker that given my experience in negotiating with lenders, I could probably be a very good commercial banker if I wanted. But no thanks, I'll stick with what I'm doing. I'm forever grateful for somehow surviving during this storm and for the people who helped along the way. I never signed up for that, but what I learned would be very valuable. My angst and frustration about our family business was also melting away as I realized that it was less about me and more about what God was doing in my life. I realized how important our business was to so many people, such as employees, subcontractors, vendors, and the communities we did business in. How tragic it would have been if we had not survived! Still, it was a tough time because we had to lay off many good employees and sell some of our idle equipment to help lower costs.

Leading up to this recession there were many times and many years that I struggled with why I was part of the family business and whether I had made the best decision by being a part of it. Ultimately, after getting through everything, and in all humility, I realized that God put me in this position ("for such a time as this" Esther 4:14) to help lead our company through that terrible time and to contribute to its survival. This is ultimately what our family business was about—working with my dad, mom, brothers, employees (who are like family to us), subcontractors, vendors, and bankers to get us through that ordeal and help us all to survive. There was no doubt in my mind after this that I had made the right decision, long ago, to join the family business, and I am still very grateful to this day. This storm healed me of any doubts and angst about being part of the family business.

We certainly have received numerous compliments from many others for our ability to survive when so many others in the industry failed. But I know that our survival was by the grace of God! Let me be dramatic and repeat: Our business survived by the grace of God! Yes, it took everything we had including lots of grit; yes, it took many small strategic steps and decisions along the way; yes, it took many others who inspired us and helped us to get through, but it was God's grace, in the end, that determined our survival. Many things fell right, and timing was everything. This had to be God's doing. By going through this storm, I learned a lot about myself and where my security comes from. It certainly didn't come from financial success, because that failed me. All financial success did was pressure me to increase it and accumulate more the next year, creating all sorts of anxiety. Instead, I learned that my true blessings come from God and my dependence on him. He is our foundation to bear all in life's storms. This is very comforting.

So, the major storm in my life had come and gone. I was looking forward to life getting back to normal. It would now be a new normal, one where I would be much more appreciative and grateful for what I had. I felt that I had had my eyes opened to seeing God working in my life and what that meant. I believed I'd witnessed him working with us for the company's survival. Yet there was something that still had me questioning the real purpose of what had happened over the last five years. Was there more to it? Surely, this storm was passing, and I would not have to experience another storm like this again for a long, long time.

Or so I thought!

CHAPTER 7:

Again?

The years 2012 into 2013 were transitional, both with our business and personally. That may sound strange, given what had transpired in the previous five years, but as the saying goes, the only thing that is constant is change. We were just coming out of arguably the worst business climate ever for our company. Our residential business had lost money in three out of the last five years, and while the commercial construction business was able to remain profitable (barely, during a couple of years), it was hardly sufficient to make up the difference. Our revenue, though, was starting to grow. Margins were still lagging from where they were before the recession, however, making it difficult to support our still-present debt service on the land that we owned. At least now we had some cash flow to help us creatively get through this time, and we continued to work out "deals" with financial lenders who now recognized us as survivors. We realized, though, that this was going to be a slow process. We were once again starting to sell and build on lots that we owned, just not at the pace before the recession. Because of all the foreclosures that had taken place during the past five years, we were competing against cheap bank-owned lots in other developments in western Wisconsin. We were walking a tightrope as our construction margins were lower than we wanted, and we were selling our lots for a lot less than we wanted. We needed the revenue for promised quarterly payments to our lenders to fulfill the workout mortgages we had negotiated. We also had undeveloped property and commercial/industrial land that we needed to make payments on. It was still a stressful time, but we had something to work with now as sales began to pick up, and we could see what we hoped would be better times ahead.

At this point, I thought about how it could have been different if we had given up and allowed our creditors to take back our property, as many other developers and builders had done. We could perhaps be clear of much of the debt we were still carrying or at least be in a stronger position to "start over." But we hadn't quit. We'd stuck with what we had agreed to with our lenders and that was to pay back whatever we had borrowed. Our integrity and character meant a lot to us, whether it was good times or bad times. We also started to pursue other banking relationships, trying to find lenders who would come alongside us to help us succeed once again.

By now I was seeing clearly that we weren't in total control of our situation. It was God's timing, and it was my responsibility to follow and trust in him as we moved forward. There were plenty of horror stories of bank foreclosures and closings all around us. Many previously successful businesses were forced to declare bankruptcy as the owners lost almost everything. I felt blessed that we were able to continue in business as we plodded along.

In November of that year, our first grandchild, Asher, was born to our daughter Lydia and her husband, Kelly. At the time, they lived in Decatur, Illinois. All grandparents know what a time of happiness and joy it is to welcome your first grandchild into this world. Jeanne made the long drive from the Twin Cities to central Illinois to be there for the birth, and I flew down a few days later. Once home from the hospital, Jeanne and I did our part to help out where we could. The house that they rented had lots of mature trees, and now in late fall, the yard was filled with a thick blanket of leaves. Jeanne and I spent the better part of a day raking and packing the leaves into some twenty-four bags. It was a labor of love, and it was our pleasure to help.

Late in the afternoon, after completing the task, I decided to go out for a late afternoon run, which I enjoyed doing. However, after starting my run, I felt this unexpected ache in my ribs and chest area. I quickly thought about my heart but realized that my breathing was fine and my heartbeat was also strong and steady. Something just didn't seem right, though. I finished my run and didn't think too much more about it, assuming that it would just go away. A month later, though, I was still dealing with this achiness in my chest and didn't have any idea what was going on. I started to wonder if it was the stress of the past few years that was finally taking a toll on me. I decided to call my good friend Jay, who was a family practice doctor in the Dallas area. Jay and I were each other's best men at our weddings and were fraternity brothers from the University of Minnesota, and we still enjoyed spending time with each other, even if it was just on the phone. As good friends do, we could always pick up where we left off! I told Jay about my ailment, and he was concerned. He said that if I were his patient presenting achiness in the chest area, he would immediately do an EKG (electrocardiogram). He convinced me that a trip to the doctor was warranted.

The doctor that I saw did indeed ask for an EKG strip, but it showed nothing abnormal. After this, and over the next few months, I did several other tests, including X-rays, ultrasounds, and an endoscopy. At this point, the doctors had no explanation. I could tell that something was off, but no one could give me an explanation. My good friend Dave, from North Carolina, even threw out the possibility that it could be scar tissue from my shoulder surgery a couple of years prior. But still, it lingered. I certainly wasn't trying to let it bother me. I thought of Philippians 4:6: "Do not be anxious about anything, but in every situation, by prayer and petition, with thanksgiving, present your requests to God." I had made up my mind that I was done with the years of stress and that, going forward, I was turning all over to God and letting him be in control of not only my business but also my personal life. That is what I tried to do then, even though something didn't feel quite right. Summer came and it was a normal fun-filled time with family, enjoying time at the cabin, water sports, and, of course, golfing. But what was that nagging achiness?

In the fall of 2013, Jeanne and I took a business trip to Lake Tahoe, which was special for us because that is where we had spent our honeymoon thirty-three years prior. We were there several days before the conference and spent much of it on hiking trails, enjoying the great scenery and the beauty of Lake Tahoe and the surrounding mountains. I was still trying to ignore the achiness that was now also in my upper back. It didn't stop me from hiking several miles in the beautiful Sierra Nevada overlooking Lake Tahoe, though.

A few weeks later I had another business trip to Arlington, Texas, for the National Association of Church Design Builders (NACDB). I was one of the leaders of the association, was on the board, and was slated to become the president the following year. However, as something didn't seem right with me, I requested that I pass on the position. I really didn't have an explanation. I'm not sure if it was my gut or my heart telling me this, or maybe, just maybe, I was finally tuning in to what God wanted and was listening to his whisper. My good friend Dave, who I previously talked about, was the current president, and he and I worked out an arrangement to continue to lead together. He would remain president, with myself as vice president. It seemed to be a good arrangement and certainly worked out that way. For me, there was no regret at passing on the president position as I had all I could comfortably deal with at the time.

Upon returning from this trip, I developed a lower gastro-intestinal (GI) tract problem and made an appointment with my gastroenterologist. Now my upper back was giving me some serious pain issues, which ended up being diagnosed as a rhom-boid muscle strain. The problem was that one day it would be in the right upper back area and the next week it would be in the left. I was starting to doubt the diagnosis and continued dealing with this pain. I had never had to deal with chronic pain before, and I was definitely learning how disabling it was. It's even harder to make good decisions when you're in pain. This was getting serious, and I was hoping to get answers soon.

My gastroenterologist, Dr. Link, was very reassuring about my GI problem. He thought it was probably an ailment called microscopic colitis and would confirm the diagnosis with a pro-cedure and some additional blood tests. The treatment ended up being quite simple and effective. I wished that I had seen him sooner, as one problem seemed to compound the stress and pain of another.

However, a couple of days after doing the bloodwork, Dr. Link called me to confirm his diagnosis but then said some-thing very unexpected. He said that the blood work revealed a high level of protein in my blood and recommended that I see a hematologist as soon as possible. I replied, "Are you telling me that you suspect that I have cancer?" He said that he suspected that it could be a blood cancer called multiple myeloma or perhaps just a preliminary ailment called MGUS (monoclonal gammopathy of unknown significance). My personal doctor called me that same day to confirm and to calm my nerves a little. He said that hematologists usually practice in cancer centers but don't assume the worst at this time. I was good with that and quite calm about this whole thing for some reason. Okay, God, you might be taking me somewhere I hadn't been planning to go but go I must.

Checking in for my first hematology appointment at the cancer center was definitely not on my bucket list. I assumed that most of the patients in the clinic either had cancer or were being diagnosed with cancer. Not me though, as I believed it was going to be something other than that. I started with my doctor's assistant, who asked me all sorts of questions about my health and any ailments that I might have. It was the most detailed triage I had ever experienced. Then I met my hematologist, who calmly explained to me that my blood markers pointed toward multiple myeloma or perhaps what is designated as smoldering multiple myeloma, but several tests would be necessary to verify the diagnosis. In one month, there were many tests, including more blood tests, urine tests, X-rays (a complete body scan of every bone in my body), and finally the most painful one of all, a bone marrow biopsy to measure the actual level of cancerous cells in my bone marrow (where the malignant plasma cells reside). This last test is one that I will never forget.

With Jeanne at my side, I went in for the bone marrow biopsy the week of Thanksgiving 2013. I'm glad that I didn't know what I was in for ahead of time. The nurse gave me a valium to relax me. I only took half because I am macho, have a high threshold for pain, and planned on returning to the office after the test.

I regretted that decision.

I laid down on the bed on my stomach while the area was prepped on my right hip bone. I was given a local shot or two of lidocaine to deaden the area, which in itself was painful and didn't seem to be that effective. At that point, the nurse took out what I perceived as the longest and thickest hollow needle I had ever seen and pushed it into my upper buttock, breaking through the hip bone into the marrow and removing the necessary amount to be analyzed. To say it was painful was an understatement. It was a combination of pressure and excruciating pain. Jeanne was on her knees with her face next to mine, encouraging me as tears streamed down my contorted face. I thought about all the patients who'd had this procedure in the past and that if they could handle it, so could I. I think, though, at this time I was starting to realize the seriousness of the situation.

Wife's Note: The nurse who performed this procedure was tentative, as though either he did not want to do this or was unsure. I determined that he was unsure and inexperienced as he could not establish the necessary route for the procedure, grinding his hip area multiple times. Watching him attempt and

re-attempt was grueling, so I chose to focus on Bill in his agony,
feeling helpless as he struggled with the pain and the length of
time it took.

The nurse apologized during and after the procedure, which
is something that he probably had become accustomed to doing.
Once I was bandaged and up off the bed, I stared at that vial of
marrow that I had just painfully given, hoping it would give me
the best of results. Even so, I was ready to hear something that
I really didn't want to hear.

We had an appointment already set with our hematologist
on the Friday after Thanksgiving, but I had asked him to call me
with the results as soon as he had them.

On Thanksgiving afternoon my cell phone vibrated, and
it was my hematologist calling me. Jeanne and I excused ourselves to our bedroom while our four adult children wondered
what was going on. He quickly and calmly confirmed that I had
multiple myeloma, a blood cancer of the plasma cells in the
bone marrow, and that he would go over other details and a plan
going forward at our appointment tomorrow. I had never heard
of this cancer before. I certainly knew of other blood cancers
like leukemia and lymphoma but had never heard of this one.
I didn't quite grasp how serious of a condition this was either,
although our research told us that immediate treatment may
not be necessary until it reached a certain level. That seemed
strange as we all think of treating cancer as quickly as possible
and trying to eradicate it from our bodies. We had much more
research to do!

After the call and later after our guests had left, we met with our children and broke the news to them. It was a family meeting like none we had had in the past. Certainly not a typical Thanksgiving family discussion. We tried to explain that, to the best of our knowledge, I was going to survive this. It was going to be monitored for the time being, without treatment until necessary, as the body can build resistance to the drugs used to treat multiple myeloma. And because the array of treatments available was still relatively small compared to other blood cancers, it was considered wise to hold off for now. Four adult children and, of course, four different reactions. There was plenty of sadness that their healthy father in his late fifties had been diagnosed with a terminal, incurable but treatable cancer that, at the time, had an average life expectancy of seven years from diagnosis. There was certainly some anger and some tears, but mostly calmness as we explained to our Christian children that God's purpose was much greater than anything else, even cancer. He had a reason and purpose for this, and now was a time for prayer, to lean on him as we tried to understand the why.

Our appointment with my doctor the next day was generally uneventful as the news was out and we'd had time to sleep on it. I believe that my doctor was quite surprised by the calmness we exhibited, given the seriousness of the situation. My calmness and hope came from the Lord at this point, and the joy of now understanding that the previous major storm had prepared me for this one. In his caring and loving kindness, God had prepared me for a much greater and much more serious storm.

My body, mind, and soul were much more ready, knowing that I now better understood the things that mattered most. I had my loving wife, Jeanne, on one side as my caretaker, and my all-loving, all-healing God on my other, ready to guide me forward. Wow, I had now gone from a conceited belief that I would get through life without a major storm to contend with, to now entering another major storm just as the other one had hardly finished! In a way, I looked forward to what lay ahead, knowing God would use this to help change me so that I could learn from it. Concerned? Perhaps. Afraid? Not really. Or at least that is what I had convinced myself and others to think.

CHAPTER 8:

Winter of Pain

C ancer. Regardless of your attitude, it is a word that you definitely don't want to hear for yourself or for a loved one! Given that it was a reality for me now, we were consumed with doing what it took to beat the odds of survival while maintaining as normal a lifestyle as possible. As I mentioned earlier, when I was diagnosed, the average life expectancy for multiple myeloma (MM) was about seven years after diagnosis. But the average is the very top of the bell curve, and I was determined to get to the other side of that curve and preferably someplace way out on the right-hand tail of the curve. Our research told us that treatments for MM were progressing very quickly, probably more than for most other cancers. My chances of survival were much better than, let's say, fifteen to twenty years earlier. Let's not sugarcoat it, though. MM is a deadly cancer, and even though I had never heard of it before my diagnosis, I was quickly becoming acquainted with it through the research we were doing. I was also learning of many famous people who had died from it and wondered how MM was not a more well-known blood cancer, like its cousins leukemia and lymphoma. We were learning that if you were going to get it, now was a better time, as it was quickly becoming a much more treatable and manageable cancer, although still incurable.

My hematologist was not prescribing treatment at this point. We would monitor my numbers (blood and urine) every month or two while we waited to see if the cancer progressed to a point where treatment was absolutely needed. This seemed counter-intuitive to what we usually see with cancer, because we are told to catch it early and then treat it as quickly as possible. But our understanding was that since the available drug treatments for treating MM were still limited, they did not want to start any earlier than necessary for fear that my body would develop resistance to the drugs. Okay, we were good with that, so let the waiting begin, we reasoned. Besides, who is really looking forward to starting cancer treatment anyway?

Early on, I resolved that cancer was not going to define who I was. Even though this diagnosis was very unexpected, the previous storm that I had just exited had prepared me in many ways for this. I was beginning to see God working in my life in more and more ways. If I truly believed that God has a purpose in all things, then I needed to try to understand. I was prepared for this—because of him. Cancer could someday kill me, but in the meantime, I refused to let it control the way I lived as much as possible. For these reasons and others, Jeanne and I decided to keep my cancer diagnosis under wraps for as long as possible. Yes, we had told our children, but I didn't want it to go much further. I guess that I didn't want it to be the talk of the family business and overly worry anyone, especially since we were coming out of one of the worst times in our company's history and had so many important decisions ahead. We wanted to deal with this on our terms and not have to deal with all the questions that might come with this diagnosis. Besides, we were still learning about the severity of this cancer and certainly weren't sure of the long-term prognosis yet. I guess I wasn't ready to talk about my cancer all the time, every day, which is what I feared would happen. Right or wrong, we didn't even tell either of our immediate families for the time being. We prayed that God would make it clear to us when the time came to open up to our family and close friends. It was tough not telling my mom and dad, but they and my siblings were dealing with Mom's Alzheimer's diagnosis and her declining health. We didn't think it was necessary to add to that and complicate our family's life at this time.

Shortly after my diagnosis, I once again called my lifelong, good friend, and retired doctor, Jay, who lived in the Dallas area. I felt that it would be a blessing for me to spend some time on the phone with him as I tried to understand what might be ahead for me. The call did not go quite as I expected. Certainly, Jay was very supportive. As a strong Christian and from his experiences as a doctor, he understood the power of prayer and that healing can happen through the work of God. He was very reassuring to me about that. However, Jay also told me that he and his wife, Lori, had just taken over custody of their one-year-old grandson, and until I called, he'd been feeling very sorry for himself because he had planned a different retirement for himself than raising a family again. Now with my news, he said that he would not want to trade places with me. He was feeling very fortunate suddenly. We helped each other realize that God's plan for our lives doesn't always go the way we envision. Each of us was now dealing with something very unexpected, although Jay admitted that raising a grandson wouldn't be all bad comparatively. As for me, I was now deep into my second storm in a very short time but realized the importance of relying on God as I sought to get through this storm, this time. I understood that control over this was not possible, but my attitude and the way I handled what I was going through could possibly help and influence others. As my call ended with Jay, he thanked me for telling him about my cancer and how I felt about it. My story and attitude were an uplifting blessing to him in his situation. Funny how something like how I deal with cancer could be a blessing to others. I was beginning to understand again how in all things, God works for the good of those who love him (a paraphrase of Romans 8:28). Let your light shine no matter what crisis you may be dealing with in life. This was a time of testing once again for my faith.

We also told our church small group members about my diagnosis. It was an important time to have that support from these important people in our lives. We needed that support as well as their continual prayer. A little bit of sympathy now and then wasn't bad either. But this rock-solid support group of fellow believers was very important in helping us maintain strength and to persevere.

The early winter months were busy with work but also with follow-up appointments at the cancer clinic. We were spending a lot of time researching and trying to understand this cancer that occupied, according to my bone marrow biopsy, 20 percent of the plasma cells in my body. The upper back pain was increasing, and it became an everyday experience for me. But not so much at this point that it prevented me from carrying out my everyday activities. Sadly, that was going to change soon. Jeanne and I were able to sneak away in late January for some time in Punta Gorda, Florida. During this time, we also had scheduled my peer group of eight contractors from around the nation to meet there for a couple of days. We had become very good friends and had met a couple of times a year for several years, helping and counseling each other with business and personal matters. This small group of men meant a lot to me, so it was very tough not to tell them directly about my cancer, but Jeanne and I wanted to keep it quiet. However, I was starting to grimace in pain when I coughed or laughed, and I suspected that a couple of them were wondering what was going on. (And, yet I didn't relate this pain to my cancer. I assumed it was a pulled muscle or something in my back.) After brunch on Sunday, my friends left, and I was looking forward to playing golf with my dad the next day on his course in North Fort Myers. However, as Jeanne and I were putting away the plastic pool cover in the garage later that afternoon, something snapped in my upper left back as I made a quick turn, and the pain just shot through my back. I relaxed as best I could, and even though I could "grin and bear it," I realized that golf was not an option with this stinging, aching pain in my upper back. It was with sadness that I called Dad and regretfully told him that I couldn't golf the next day. Understand how big a deal that was: I love golf a lot, and it was not like me to cancel a round. I'm sure my dad was probably wondering what was going on, even though it was well-known that I was plagued by upper back pain.

When we returned home, I saw my doctor about my pain and again determined that it was probably an upper back muscle injury. Since X-rays did not give any answers, he prescribed physical therapy for me twice a week. I was very grateful to my therapist because his massaging and taping of my back seemed to give some short-term relief, but typically by the next appointment, the pain would be returning. At the office, I kept a warm heating pad on my chair back to help with the pain. Slowly over the next month, it seemed to be getting better. So much so that I planned on easing back into golf again on our three-week trip to Florida in March.

The first week of our time away in Florida was a business conference at Disney World. My back was starting to feel much better, and it was great to walk around in the warm Florida air for the first few days. However, within a few days of being there, and probably due to all the standing and walking, my upper back, especially over the left shoulder blade, started to ache again. I reasoned that I'd probably overdone it and after a few days of rest, I would be good again. However, at the end of the conference, we volunteered to take some friends of ours to the Orlando airport before we headed south to Punta Gorda for the rest of our vacation. As I was helping to lift one of their suitcases out of the trunk of our car, I felt that zinging pain across my upper back once again. The pain was back with a vengeance! It was a painful two-hour trip back to our place, but I looked forward to easing the pain with rest. However, it would not abate, at least not much. I would sleep okay, but in the morning, when I got up, I could feel the pain settle again into my upper back. My morning treatment was Advil, a warm shower, and sitting in the recliner for a couple of hours reading while enjoying a cup of coffee until I felt better. I believe that my dad was starting to wonder what was going on as I once again was unavailable for golf. I became good at hiding the pain as long as I didn't have to cough or laugh! Keep in mind that I did not relate this pain to my cancer and saw it as a temporary back issue of some type.

Out of desperation, we even made a couple of appointments for physical therapy during our stay in Punta Gorda. The therapist examined my symptoms and asked if I had been in a serious car accident, as I was presenting the type of pain symptoms that he saw with his car accident patients. The couple of sessions I had with him certainly helped me, but the ever-present pain was still haunting me.

It was at this time that Jeanne looked at me and asked that if she called Mayo Clinic and was able to get an appointment for me, would I go? I questioned what a second opinion would do as I already knew that I had multiple myeloma. She was very insistent, especially with the pain that I was experiencing. She was truly concerned for me and felt that we had to go somewhere for answers. I agreed. When we got home in late March, she called the Mayo Clinic number and after a long conversation and being put on hold several times, she secured an appointment for the first week in June. Wow, that was quick, I thought. I heard that most people wait months to get an appointment at Mayo Clinic. Evidently, they wanted to see me!

I continued my physical therapy with my therapist well into May. *He* even seemed to be frustrated with the lack of progress I was making. He was starting to feel that I might have a thoracic disc issue and was thinking of referring me to an orthopedic doctor. However, the pain once again started to ease in May. Finally, some relief! Thank you, God, for healing me. I wasn't sure why I was going through all this pain and dealing with cancer, but I knew that he was there and there was a reason. What that was, had yet to be revealed. But what a winter of pain it had been, and I was certainly ready for relief and healing.

This season in my life was teaching me empathy for those people who deal with chronic pain in their lives. It was certainly making my life a lot tougher. Making decisions while you are dealing with pain is much more difficult. I had days at the office when I didn't have a clear enough mind to deal with the work or decisions that lay in front of me. And in hindsight, this pain probably blinded me from asking the right questions of my doctors about what was really going on. Instead, every time the pain reared its ugly head, I was able to explain it away with something that I had done, either overexertion, lifting, or something like that. For that reason, Jeanne has said that, looking back, this was more than a time of pain but also a time of misunderstanding. The answers would hopefully come from Mayo Clinic. In the meantime, I tried to keep a smile on my face with as good an attitude as possible while having faith that this too would pass.

Answers and Faith

Most people know that Mayo Clinic is in Rochester, the third-largest city in Minnesota. Mayo Clinic dominates the city and is far and away the largest employer, with over forty thousand employees. It consistently ranks as one of the top, if not *the* top, medical clinics and hospitals in most major medical fields. It was a privilege to have such a top-notch facility located less than ninety minutes from our home. Downtown Rochester is seemingly dominated by the Mayo Clinic. Multistory buildings rise for several blocks to house all the staff, equipment, and patients. Celebrities and important people from all over the world come to be seen by the Mayo staff for their medical needs. In early June 2014, I became a patient and received my Mayo Clinic number just like every other patient who goes to the clinic.

A lot had changed for me in the last few years. The Great Recession had quite an effect on me. I had learned to team up my smart business sense with a renewed heart for God. Instead of acting solely when I believed it was time to take action, I had now become much more in tune with the thoughts and ideas of others while trying to balance growth for our company with my ambition for success. One of my God-given strengths was the ability and willingness to take the proper action at the right time. This brings me to this moment in time as we entered Mayo Clinic. We knew that something wasn't right and thanks to Jeanne taking action, we were there to hopefully find some answers.

Jeanne had compiled and organized all my necessary medical records as requested by Mayo Clinic. They wanted to know everything about me. My first scheduled stop was to Internal Medicine for a physical exam. I was assigned to see Dr. Lundstrom, an older, very experienced, and very kind physician. The first surprise was when they weighed me and measured my height. They used the metric system, so when the nurse told me my height, I asked her to convert it to feet and inches. When she said, "Five feet nine inches," I said, "No, that can't be right. I may not be exactly five eleven, but I am pretty close to that." She looked at me and said that five feet nine was correct. We were very puzzled by that. Dr. Lundstrom was very pleasant, and we enjoyed our time with him. He took as long as possible to answer our questions and fill in the blanks for us. At that point, it was off to the lab to have several vials of blood drawn, and we would follow up with him tomorrow. As we were going over my results the next day, Dr. Lundstrom (who was a cancer survivor himself) started talking about multiple myeloma and that he had a good friend on the West Coast who developed a pain in his back seemingly overnight. He explained that multiple myeloma has a way of just dropping in on you. One day you feel fine, and the next day you have an unexplained ache or pain. As he said that, I thought back to November of 2012, when I suddenly had that ache and discomfort in my ribs and upper back. It was now clear to me that was when I first felt the effects of multiple myeloma. An answer to one of my many questions.

Thank you, Lord.

The rest of the test results pointed out that I was quite healthy, perhaps a little overweight with slightly above-normal blood pressure, except for the incurable cancer that was roaming around in my body. That afternoon, we would be meeting with our hematologist, Dr. Morie Gertz. Dr. Lundstrom asked if I knew anything about him and I just shrugged my shoulders. He explained that Dr. Gertz was not only well-known nationally as an expert multiple myeloma hematologist but that he also served as head of Internal Medicine for Mayo Clinic. Once again, I believe that God must have had his hand in making sure that I received care from someone of Dr. Gertz's stature.

Jeanne and I made our first trip to the tenth floor of the Mayo building where Hematology is located. Little did we know at that time how many more trips we would be making to Mayo 10, and still make to this day. We were taken back to one of the exam rooms that Dr. Gertz uses, and after having my weight, height, and vitals taken, we sat on the couch in the room for the patient and caregiver (that was the new term that I learned for Jeanne). There was a knock on the door and in came this distinguished-looking doctor, in a suit and tie, who greeted us by saying, "Good afternoon, Mr. and Mrs. Derrick. It is good to meet you." My initial impression was that he wasn't one for small talk and wanted to get down to business. Our conversation was straightforward, and he was very direct. He asked me to explain the pain I was having and how long I'd had it. At that point, he told me to hop on the exam table and he did a thorough exam. When he was done, he told me that I could sit up. As he watched me grimace when I painfully came to a sitting position, he leaned back up against the wall opposite the table. Dr. Gertz without hesitation asked, "Have you done any research on multiple myeloma?" At this point, I was feeling a little insulted. Of course, we had, as it seemed like that was all the reading either of us was doing. "So, you know about the relationship between myeloma and pain?" I sheepishly said, "Of course." He then said that I was presenting classic symptoms of pain related to myeloma. He was convinced that what was going on in my back was related to my cancer and that we were going to do a scan and find it. Jeanne was very pleased to hear that and said that it was about time someone ordered an MRI of my back. Dr. Gertz said, "Oh no, not an MRI." He was ordering a PET (positron emission tomography) scan of my entire body from the top of my head to my kneecaps. We would meet with him the next day to review the results as soon as they were available. I was beginning to question how seriously we had taken this disease.

Things happen quickly at Mayo, whether it is getting simple lab tests or scheduling diagnostic tests like a PET scan. My scan was immediately scheduled, and within twenty-four hours I was being prepped for the scan as a technician injected a radioactive fluid into me that would be absorbed by my body. After sitting quietly for an hour, I was ushered into this room that had a large piece of equipment. I was strapped onto the table of the machine and within minutes, into the machine I went. My first scan at Mayo Clinic but certainly not my last! The next day, we met with Dr. Gertz to go over the results of the scan. He explained that with a PET scan, any areas that had abnormally growing cells would "light up," indicating that cancer cells were present in that location. He turned his large color monitor toward us as he started working his way from my head downward. Relief came when he mentioned that I had a normal brain scan. Then he started showing us a series of slides starting at the top of my neck and working his way down my upper back. All was looking normal until he got to thoracic disc number 3, where he pointed out that the very bottom was showing some color. He of course knew what was coming next, and he clicked to the next slide, which was the T4 disc right between my shoulder blades. It lit up with color, and he said that there was the source of my pain. It was technically called *plasmacytoma*, better known to us laypeople as a malignant tumor located in my T4 disc. He quickly went through the rest of the scan results, which showed nothing else of concern. But back to the tumor. To say that Jeanne and I were shocked was an understatement. I believe that this was more of a shock to us than my original diagnosis! This made the cancer I had much more real. I asked how it would be treated. Would it require surgery to remove it? Dr. Gertz said absolutely not, as the tumor was up against my spinal cord, and it would be far too risky to remove it with surgery. He said that chemotherapy would be an option but believed that radiation therapy would be best to eliminate the tumor as quickly as possible. We asked how soon we should start radiation, and he said tomorrow would be good! In other words, this was extremely serious with the location of the tumor adjacent to my spinal cord. He said that until the radiation was completed, he wanted me to take it easy—no lifting, no twisting, no excessive bending, and certainly no golfing! Even though this was only the second appointment with Dr. Gertz, I could genuinely feel his concern for my immediate well-being. He inferred that until treated, paralysis was a concern. He certainly had our attention.

Now a moment of reflection is in order. Remember how the pain in my back had prevented me from golfing while on vacation in Florida not once but twice that past winter? It also prevented me from other activities I would do with the onset of warmer weather, such as waterskiing. I now believe that God had sent the pain to protect me from hurting myself. No one will ever be able to convince me that this wasn't the work of God in my life. I am so grateful for his protection during this time. Jeanne's frustration with my condition may have helped persuade her to get me an appointment at Mayo Clinic, but I also know that she was led by the Holy Spirit along the way. We finally had our answer, although it certainly wasn't what we expected. But I was starting to get used to the unexpected. I have to wonder how often God tries to send us a message but we're too busy with the noise of life to listen. Sometimes it does take a whack upside the head to get the message!

After making the decision to be treated at Mayo Clinic going forward, I was scheduled for an MRI scan of my upper body using dye to clearly see the location for the radiation treatment and the damage that was done by this malignancy. The next morning, we met with the radiologist who showed us the results of the scan. Another surprise. We could see the T3 disc and the T5 disc, but there was very little in between where the T4 disc should have been. The tumor had been eating away at my disc, weakening it and causing a compression fracture that was the source of my pain. It also explained why I was so much shorter now than I used to be. All this had been going on during this time that I was in pain. I was not bitter about it not being found sooner, but rather I felt a sense of relief, now knowing the reason for my pain. It certainly reinforced the seriousness of my situation, but I felt secure being treated at Mayo Clinic. I knew that God was also looking out for me, and for that reason alone, I wasn't too worried about what lay ahead. Concerned, but not too worried. As far as my compressed and fractured disc was concerned, there would be no plans to repair it and instead we would just allow scar tissue and natural healing to take place once the tumor was radiated away.

Everything continued at a fast pace. In the afternoon, I was fitted with my radiation "mask." It was a thin sheet of fiberglass that was moistened with hot water and form-fitted to my face and head and then snapped to the radiation table to help hold my upper body still during the radiation. Then the machine was programmed for the exact location for the radiation, and a tiny ink dot was placed on my chest in that location. I would receive five sessions of radiation starting the next day. I repeat, this was all happening so quickly! A week before, we would have never guessed what was going to happen in one week. Finally, we went to the scheduling desk to schedule my radiation sessions. We worked around my work schedule, or should I say, my work schedule worked around the radiation sessions. Certainly, my priorities continued to be shifted around yet again.

The next day we made the ninety-minute drive to Mayo Clinic. I believe that I was quite silent about what might lay ahead. Jeanne would attest that I am never too talkative when driving, but this drive was different as I thought about what was going to happen that day. Life was changing for us very quickly. We checked in at the "subway" level of the Charlton building where Radiation was located. As I waited in the lobby, I looked around at the other patients who were waiting and realized that as bad as our own situation might be, one can always find someone who is worse off. There were many right there in the waiting room. Not all of them were able to walk in as I was. I struck up a conversation with the gentleman in the chair across from me, and he said that he was getting forty-plus radiation sessions on his leg! I felt bad when I told him that I was only receiving five sessions. How fortunate I truly was.

My name was called, and I kissed Jeanne and muttered, "Here I go," before rising out of the chair to follow the nurse through the door and into a big room filled with a large piece of equipment. There were technicians in the room who helped me lay down on the right spot on the table, and then I was fastened in. Next, my mask was placed over my head and fastened to the table. I guessed that it was too late to turn back now. The technicians placed the table in approximately the right location, and the machine's "autopilot" made the final adjustments so that radiation would go through my body at the exact location of the tumor. At this point, the technicians exited the room, leaving me alone with the radiation equipment. There was a TV monitor high on the wall in front of me, and it had a moving outdoor scene with swaying grass, a small stream of water, and trees in the background. I noticed it but at this point, my eyes were "looking through the building" at the sky, and as the machine hummed, I tried to pray. What came out was, "Lord, I am no longer driving. I am along for the ride. Take me where you want me to go, and give me the courage to follow." I'm not sure that I could say I had an "out of body" experience, but I feel like at that very moment, my faith went from my head to my heart. I certainly was no longer in control, and I was very thankful to the One who was. Was this a moment of conversion? I was already a follower of Christ, but it was certainly a moment of my faith being deepened like never before.

From the time my name was called to the time I returned to the waiting lobby, approximately fifteen minutes elapsed, but based on my experience, it seemed much longer. I truly felt like a lot happened to me during that short period of time. I repeated the process the following week for four more days, and then I was done. Before I left the Radiation lobby after my last session, I had the privilege to go over to the wall where this good-sized bell hung. All radiation therapy patients get to ring that bell after their last session to signify being done. I was not going to be denied. I grabbed the rope hanging from the bell and, with a smile, gave it a couple of good tugs. Everyone in the waiting room knew what that meant, and after I rang the bell, clapping and cheers followed. It was a moment that brought tears to my eyes.

My follow-up appointment with Dr. Gertz went well. He was pleased with the results and my follow-up tests confirmed that my tumor was eradicated. The lingering pain in my upper back that extended into my left shoulder blade was still there, but that too would eventually get better. Yes, the radiation had zapped me of my energy, but that would slowly start to return. I had a square "sunburn" patch on my back where the radiation had entered my body and a similar square on my chest where it had escaped. Other than that, I recovered very well from this adventure.

Jeanne and I knew that it was time to tell our families what was going on. As if they didn't suspect something already. I took my dad to lunch and told him that I had cancer but not to worry about me because I was in good shape, and I was going to beat it. He took it very calmly and didn't seem to show too much concern. I believe that his concern and emotion were being spent on our mom who was at a small memory care home in New Richmond. My brothers and sister all were very supportive and empathetic, of course, and wanted to help in any way they could. My brother Ron especially empathized with me, as he had successfully battled and defeated a very deadly muscle cancer while in college many years before. He certainly understood, even though I felt his battle was much worse than mine. I went and visited Mom to tell her what I was battling and felt she probably didn't realize what I was saying. That was okay, I didn't need her to worry about me anyway. Perhaps, though, deep in her mind she understood and was praying for her oldest son.

We started to actively share with others about the cancer. As a business leader in the community, the word spread quickly. Although I appreciated the sympathy and care shown to me, I didn't have time for any pity parties. I had a life to live. Not just my life but the life that God wanted me to live, whatever that was. I felt right then that I needed to go about the business of figuring out what that was or what that meant. It was time for me to not only learn to live with cancer but also help lead our business after escaping disaster during the recession. Our business and I had survived. Now it was time to thrive!

And I knew that God would be there.

CHAPTER 10:

In Between

I was now entering a time of in-between. I was in between being diagnosed with an incurable cancer and my initial radiation treatment and where it would take me next. I was learning to live with cancer. This was a period of time in my life that ended up lasting about eighteen months and was packed with many experiences. I knew that I was traveling toward some sort of chemotherapy eventually but wanted to put off the inevitable as long as I could. In all honesty, I probably was still in denial that chemo would be necessary, at least for a long, long time! But whatever time I had until treatment was necessary, I wanted to use it wisely. I would be grateful for whatever came my way. In the meantime, regular visits to Mayo 10 for lab tests were necessary to monitor the different levels that are measured to see if and how quickly the myeloma in my body was progressing. At every visit, it seemed like my blood markers would creep up a little more. Dr. Gertz kept a watchful and caring eye on this and how I was doing. I appreciated the experience that he brought with him to our regular appointments.

It was during this time in 2015 that I started to document Bible readings and devotionals that I read. Some would call this journaling, but I called it "Bill's Writings." On those days when I was truly inspired by what I had read and how it related to where I was in life, I wrote the meaning of what I read and how it applied to me. This was therapeutic for me, as I applied God's Word and the wisdom of others to my current situation. I read about Old Testament men like Jacob and Joseph, who kept their faith in God and had to wait patiently for God's timing before they were delivered for the purpose God had intended for them. *Trust, patience, purpose.* These words seemed to be a recurring theme for me at this time. I didn't know what was in store for me, but I knew that I needed to continue to trust God for my health and what may lay ahead. I was starting to realize the importance of doing God's will and trying to determine what his purpose was for me as I traveled through what seemed like a never-ending storm. Like most people, I searched to understand his purpose, but in some way, the search *is* the purpose as we try our best to trust in God for all things.

In previous chapters, I pointed out that God can speak to us through other people in our lives. It was during this time that he brought new people to me who helped me on my journey. One of these people was Kirk. Kirk lived in a city just outside the Twin Cities, and we were introduced to each other when his daughter and our youngest daughter, Shelby, became friends while attending Drake University and realized both their fathers had been diagnosed with multiple myeloma. Kirk had a more aggressive form and was going through serious chemo treatment about the time that I had been diagnosed. His situation was certainly worse than mine, but you would never know it, as his attitude of positivity and his love of the Lord were infectious. No matter what he was going through, he always put a positive spin on it. We both had the gift of gab, and our visits were never short of conversation. I made a point of visiting him whenever possible, especially those times when he was in the hospital getting extensive chemo treatments. He tried to prepare me for what might lie ahead for me. He was always encouraging. Once when we had an appointment at Mayo Clinic, he was also there recovering from a stem cell transplant and staying at the Gift of Life Transplant House. He invited us over, and even though he was not feeling the best, he showed us around in case I ever had to have a transplant (which I highly doubted at the time). He was always available to talk and encourage. It was a blessing to have Kirk as a friend during this time.

Tom Brokaw, the retired NBC anchor, was also diagnosed with multiple myeloma in 2013. He, though, was diagnosed during a routine trip to Mayo Clinic by my hematologist, Dr. Gertz. Because of this common thread, I felt a connection with him and what he detailed in his book *A Lucky Life Interrupted*, a memoir about his first year dealing with blood cancer. His book and his one-hour *Dateline* special helped me to better understand my situation. Even though I haven't had a chance to meet him, I appreciate all that he has done for me and others as he journaled and documented what he has gone through.

It was during this time that Jeanne and I were invited by friends to be their guests at the Teen Challenge fundraiser banquet in Minneapolis. To my surprise and delight, Vince Miller and his wife were also at our table. Vince, you will remember, is the pastor who'd given the sermon a few years earlier that helped to guide me after our financial storm arrived. After dinner, I took a couple of minutes and told Vince that I had started writing my story and that he had a part in it. We scheduled a time to meet for lunch and discuss why. At lunch, I told him about what a difference his sermon on building our lives on a solid foundation had made in my life. I'm not sure if he remembered giving that sermon, but he appreciated that he had made a difference. It was at this time that we became friends. He then told me about the new men's ministry he had started called Resolute. He invited me to be part of a weekly small group, called a cohort, that was going through a curriculum on how men can be better husbands, fathers, and leaders by using God's words in Scripture. At Vince's encouragement, I briefly told my story of fighting through the Great Recession and now cancer and how I was learning to trust in God through it all. I became very close with several men in this group and several of us still meet weekly, offering encouragement and accountability to each other.

95

At my regular checkups at Mayo, we would often take a break to get something to eat at the cafeteria. On one visit, the cafeteria was especially crowded, so we asked a gentleman who was by himself at a table if he would allow us to join him. He said sure, and we proceeded to get to know each other. Mike was from Racine, Wisconsin, and was battling a blood disease called *primary amyloidosis*. He had been in remission after a stem cell transplant in 2010, but now it was back, and he was at Mayo for treatment. Mike was very forthcoming about what he went through and what he was experiencing now. He had just recently retired from his accounting firm so he could do what was necessary to fight this disease that was battling him. We exchanged phone numbers and information, and he offered to help me with any questions that I might have in the future. Especially if I needed to do a stem cell transplant. I wondered why people kept bringing this up. I was not planning on needing a stem cell transplant any time soon. Mike was a godsend to me over the next couple of years, encouraging me and helping me along my journey.

Greg and his wife, Mary, were friends of ours from church. But when Greg found out from Mary via Jeanne that I had cancer, he reached out to me, and we started a routine of meeting for breakfast. Greg has a strong faith in Christ, and he became a great encourager, listener, and prayer warrior for me. Most importantly, he became a close friend of mine during this time of need. He probably doesn't realize how much our relationship has meant to me during my time in the storm. As Mary has a form of leukemia, we also had that bond of understanding what life was like living with blood cancer.

As I write this chapter, I better understand God's gift of bringing people into our lives at the right time to help us through times of need. It was like he was setting up a support group for me that would help me through the trials ahead, which at this time I was unaware of or refused to acknowledge. It was necessary for me to understand that I needed the help and support of others and to be willing to accept it. We need to recognize that God speaks to us through these people as they become a special part of our lives. If we are to understand our purpose in life, especially during our trials, people need people. I was beginning to understand that. It is important to embrace that and be grateful, and then to be there when they need someone. I could no longer be a bystander.

I now had more sense of urgency and gratitude for my work. I tried to be the best leader that I could be, perhaps using the patience and humility that God was teaching me with the trials that I was going through. I was still frustrated from time to time with the multiple leadership roles our family business had, but I was also trying to better understand my role and do the best that I could to help meet the long-term goals of our company. I spent a fair amount of time with Alan, our financial advisor, and Tim, our business advisor, trying to understand where I fit. They pointed out that even though we were related, we all had different experiences and educations and therefore different desires and expectations. I, especially, with my experience with other businesses before joining the family business, had a totally different business background. But they helped me understand and think about what my partners and the business needed from me at this time. To be an effective leader I needed to humbly accept this and be ready to help make the business decisions that needed to be made. I was learning to be a supportive leader for our business, which allowed my partners to do their jobs better and more efficiently. Tim became my coach and mentor. He helped me with many things, both personal and professional. He helped me understand how my smart business mind and my heart for God could truly make a difference in the lives of others. He helped me understand that there is a delicate balance between growth and ambition. My ability and willingness to act at the right time needed to be for the right reasons. This was a time of new growth for our company. I was starting to learn what contentment felt like.

Then in November of 2015, Dr. Gertz showed Jeanne and me my rising "numbers" as my Mspike was now at 4.0. This test determines the amount of protein in your blood that comes from the malignant cancer cells. Someone without MM would have no M-spike. That, coupled with other blood markers, he said with a concerned and caring look, meant it was time to start treatment. My time of "in-between" was about to end. A new uncharted adventure lay ahead, and I prayed to God that I would be ready and that he would guide and protect me. I was confident that he would.

CHAPTER 11:

Treatment; Not That Easy

"It was time for treatment," meaning that it was time for chemotherapy. It was time to put those nasty chemicals into my body to fight the cancer cells that were becoming stronger and stronger. I was somewhat in a daze when Dr. Gertz told me this. It was almost as if what he was telling me wasn't registering. As it slowly sunk in, I finally asked, "What's next?" I was beginning to understand that each case and individual is different. Yes, there are standard go-to treatments, but my team considered many things before recommending my specific treatment. There was a trial available for a three-drug treatment using a relatively new drug. I was randomly chosen to go ahead with the trial which meant that the drug would be provided without charge by the manufacturer, and I (my insurance) would pay for the cost of the infusion. I would receive the three-hour infusion twice a week on Thursday and Friday for three weeks in a row, and then I would get one week off. This four-week "cycle," as they were called, would be repeated every month. Along with this infusion of Kyprolis, I would be taking a chemotherapy pill called Revlimid twenty-one days on and seven days off, plus ten tablets of a steroid called dexamethasone once a week. This three-drug combination would continue for several months to hopefully bring my cancer into remission.

My chemo nurse met with Jeanne and me to go over Revlimid and the different side effects that I could experience. The list was long. One of the more curious effects he talked about was that I might experience leg cramps more often, and he asked if I knew how to counteract them. When I asked how, he said, "Pickle juice!" We have kept a jar of dill pickles in our refrigerator ever since. One of the more serious possible side effects of Revlimid is potential blood clots in the legs. To help prevent that I would be taking a regular strength aspirin as long as I was on Revlimid. In the first few months, I had a couple of false alarms, but an ultrasound of my leg proved that I was just fine.

The "Dex" as it is called, is a steroid to help fight inflammation, and its side effect was boosting one's energy to the point of having difficulty sleeping. I would take it on Thursdays at night before I went to bed and sleep just fine until three or four in the morning, but then I was awake looking for something to do. I would be that way for a couple of days, and then I would "crash" sometime on Saturday! I can imagine how much fun I was to live with.

December 23, 2015, was my first chemotherapy infusion of the drug Kyprolis (carfilzomib). We went to the tenth floor of the Gonda Building at Mayo Clinic where chemotherapy was administered. Jeanne and I were led to one of the rooms, and I sat in this very comfortable chair that would recline to any position I wanted just by the push of a button. I needed one of these at home to watch TV! Considering the circumstances, I was very calm about what was about to happen. It was what I had to do, and by now I had developed a very high level of trust with my doctors and nurses at Mayo Clinic. The nurse came in and put the IV needle into the back of my left hand (at this point I was very used to having needles put into my veins), and I was hooked up to two bags, one with my medication and one with saline solution to keep me hydrated. With a click of the valve on the tube, I started receiving my first dose of chemotherapy medicine. Not a bucket list item, for sure, but a very momentous occasion indeed in my fight with cancer. During this three-plus hour infusion, I could work, watch TV, read, get up and walk around, and get snacks or something to drink. You are treated very well by the nurses and staff while you are there. There wasn't much fanfare when I was done. I was unhooked, and Jeanne and I drove home to finish our plans for Christmas, as we weren't going to let this stand in the way of a wonderful holiday.

The next day was Christmas Eve, and while everyone was preparing for Christmas, I made the drive back to Rochester to receive my second dose of chemo in the early afternoon. Our youngest daughter, Shelby, who was home from pharmacy school, accompanied me so that Jeanne could finish up the last-minute plans for the holiday. I can honestly say that I don't ever remember "closing up" a bar in my lifetime, but I can say that I was the last patient in the chemo department that day. It was about three thirty in the afternoon when the final drips of the carfilzomib went into my vein. As the IV was being removed from the back of my hand, Shelby, I, and the two nurses attending to me that day were the only ones left on the floor! I thanked them for staying late and wished them a Merry Christmas. Shelby and I left and began the two-plus hour drive to Jeanne's family's annual Christmas Eve dinner and birthday celebration for her sister Jo, whose birthday was December 25. As we celebrated that night, I remember feeling a little bit like an island. I was going through something very different and difficult. I know that my family loved and cared for me, but we couldn't let my treatment and cancer stand in the way of celebrating this holiday. Yet it was hard to get my mind off what had happened the last couple of days and what lay ahead for me.

As if by divine design (I guess that it probably was), the Christmas church service couldn't have come at a better time for me. Thinking about what my Lord and Savior had done for me by coming to Earth was overwhelming as I asked for not only spiritual healing but also physical healing. I teared up quite a bit during that service, but the squeeze of Jeanne's hand and having Michael, Lydia, Wesley, and Shelby there meant so much to me. Even though I didn't know what might be ahead, I realized that God and my family would be there to help me through it.

Jeanne and I made the journey to Mayo Clinic every Thursday and Friday for three weeks for my first cycle of chemotherapy sessions. My health was monitored very closely by the nurses, and my comfort (including warm blankets) was also a priority to them. It wasn't too far into my treatments that I started feeling tingling in my fingertips and toes, which is called *peripheral neuropathy* and regularly happens with chemotherapy. I wasn't thrilled about it but I knew it was a possibility, even though I was hoping that it wouldn't happen! After the first three weeks, my usual blood tests were taken and showed that my treatments were working, as my M-spike had dropped considerably. This was great news. Unfortunately, during my second cycle of treatments, the side effects that I had started experiencing became more severe. There was a lot of fatigue, especially on Friday night after my second infusion of the week, and I would start spiking a fever into the night and the next morning. This was not the reaction that I expected. One Saturday, during the night, I had a fever over 102 degrees and labored breathing. Finally, at sunrise, Jeanne, with the help of our oldest son, Michael, rushed me to our local emergency room because my temperature was still high. We were concerned about an infection of some kind which can often happen during chemo because the body is in a weakened state. We were quite concerned, however after blood tests and X-rays, it was not an infection (pneumonia or otherwise), and my Mayo staff felt that it was chemo related. The realization set in that I was going to have to learn to live with this as the chemo successfully fought the cancer and my body dealt with the chemo.

The Revlimid also gave me a very uncomfortable rash on my torso, arms, and legs. The dosage was varied and sometimes I would be taken off Revlimid for a short time to recover. My body seemed to learn to tolerate the Revlimid much better as time went on, and I was able to control it better with allergy medication and antihistamines.

However, I also noticed that my right forearm into my right hand was getting weaker. I also felt more tingling in my right foot, as well as weakness. The left hand and foot had minor tingling. This was puzzling as chemo-induced neuropathy typically is symmetrical, in both hands or feet to the same degree. But this was predominately happening on my right side. I was having trouble signing my name or typing on the computer. In a short time, my right hand became extremely weak, and my fingers started to curl up. It was getting so bad that if I put my hand in my pocket, I couldn't tell if there was anything in it. The weakness was getting so bad that I couldn't zip a zipper or button a shirt with my right hand. And yes, I am right-handed, which made this especially tough.

I continued to try to work through this as best as I could. Because I couldn't use my right hand for typing, I had to resort to the "hunt and peck" method to type and eventually acquired voice-activated software to dictate my work at the office. I certainly leaned on my assistant and others to help me get my necessary paperwork done. It was slower and harder but manageable. My brothers and the entire staff were tolerant and empathetic to my situation. I still wanted to prove that I could fight cancer and competently perform my work duties as well. I tried to always keep a cheerful face, remembering that the one thing that I could control was my *attitude*. I remember one of our managers at work stopping me one day and telling me that he was amazed by my attitude, considering what I was going through. I nonchalantly asked what choice I had. He responded that I did have a choice, that he was proud of me for being so positive, that I was an inspiration to everyone, and that my battle was lifting the spirits of our team. Wow! Certainly a lesson to be learned there. During these times of crisis in our lives, others are watching us and how we handle these crises. We can be inspiring to others without even saying a word.

My chemo treatments continued, but in early March, my doctor referred me to Neurology to further diagnose what the problem was and how I could be treated. By this time, I not only didn't have the use of my right hand, but I was also walking with a limp as I was developing what is referred to as "drop foot" in my right foot. This was becoming a harder journey than I'd anticipated. After an initial examination and testing by one neurologist, I was referred to another neurologist and there were more tests. A couple of EMGs (electromyography), two spinal taps, another PET scan, a CT (computed tomography) scan, and other assorted tests were, in the scheme of things, tolerable, but I could have done without the second spinal tap. All in all, I was at Mayo Clinic five out of six days in early March for various tests, examinations, and consultations while the Neurology and Hematology departments worked together to determine the cause and how to treat it. I was still trying to receive chemo treatments through all this, but it was becoming more hit and miss. At this point, my attitude was shaky and emotional as I wondered if I would be like this for the rest of my life. Yet I just believed something good would eventually happen.

While at Mayo in early March, we found out that my friend Kirk, whom I talked about earlier, was there getting the same chemo treatment that I was receiving. Jeanne and I used that opportunity to go up and visit him. We enjoyed our time together, and I am sure glad we took the time to visit, because within a few days, he developed a viral, bacterial, and fungal infection and shockingly passed away at the end of the following week, just ten days after we'd seen him. I had no idea that was going to be the last time I saw him! Life is fragile, and we don't know what the next day may hold for us. Take the time to stay in touch with your friends and loved ones because we just don't know. Kirk's death was also a reminder to me of the seriousness of what I was dealing with, and Jeanne and I reacted to this loss dramatically and with shock.

Within a week of the barrage of tests that I'd taken, Dr. Tracy, my neurologist, called and wanted to start treatment with a steroid to help my hands and feet. It would be an infusion for five consecutive days at Mayo's infusion center, which is open 24/7. But before the fourth treatment, I reported that there was very little difference as I felt like my right hand was worse. Dr.

Tracy was called, and she canceled the remaining treatments and ordered an MRI of my leg and another PET scan for the following day while they tried to determine what would be the best course of action.

In a few days, Dr. Tracy recommended a five-day intravenous immunoglobulin therapy (IVIg) treatment of Privigen that was scheduled to start on Saturday, April 2. This immunoglobulin product was made from blood plasma and was administered by IV over three hours, and I was closely monitored by the nurses for any adverse side effects. I was put in a room with a very comfortable hospital bed in the infusion center at Methodist Hospital on the Mayo campus. It was not unusual for me to doze off during these treatments as Jeanne and the nurses took good care of me. By the fourth treatment, I was feeling much better. I was getting the use of my right hand back again and my limp was going away. After the five-day treatment, I felt so much better. It was a miracle. At one point I had resigned myself to the reality that I may not get regular use of my right hand back, but once again I felt like I was experiencing the healing power of God in addition to good medical care.

The day after my last IVIg treatment, I was back at the Mayo Clinic chemo floor restarting my two-a-week treatments that had been suspended. This lasted for two weeks, and then Jeanne and I took a group trip to Europe that included a couple of days in Paris and a week-long riverboat ride down the Rhine River from Switzerland to Amsterdam. This was my first trip to Europe, and it couldn't have come at a better time with all that was going on with my health. Because of this trip, I caught the bug for international travel and have enjoyed several trips since then. Unfortunately, during this trip the relief that the IVIg treatment had given me started to wear off. It began with my fingers starting to tingle again and then numbness started setting in, with my grip strength and dexterity affected. I was determined not to let this affect my trip, but I was concerned as I thought about what might lay ahead once we returned home.

The first week of May, we traveled back to Mayo Clinic for my chemo treatments on Thursday and Friday. I also was showing the signs of a cold coming on, probably from international travel, I guessed. By Saturday, though, I was coughing and had a fever, and on Sunday, Mother's Day, I was a mess with light-headedness, shortness of breath, and coughing up some blood. From here things started to happen fast. On Monday, my local doctor treated me for pneumonia, and on Wednesday, Dr. Tracy, my Mayo Clinic neurologist examined me. She said that she was going to contact Dr. Gertz and recommend that we stop the trial we were on. She was also going to schedule me for another five-day IVIg infusion for the numbness and weakness in my hands and feet, especially on the right side. The next day we got word that I was off the trial, which meant no more carfilzomib. We were disappointed, as it was effective on the myeloma but had become very toxic for my body. For the time being, I would stay with the Revlimid and dexamethasone and monitor my blood work regularly. And once I completed my current twenty-one-day cycle of Revlimid, they would raise my dosage in early June from 15 mg to 25 mg daily.

In the meantime, while this roller coaster was going on with my health, I was still doing my best to provide the leadership I was responsible for at our company. It was certainly difficult with all the trips to Mayo Clinic, the tests, treatments, and not feeling well on the weekends. I had a lot of time during treatments and tests to reflect on what was going on. The first six months of 2016 certainly had not transpired the way we thought they would. Even with all that I had to deal with, our commercial construction company was having one of its best years ever, reinforcing the fact that we had a very good team. This time in and out of the office allowed me to see that they were ready to lead the charge even though I wasn't there all the time. I had learned through dealing with this storm that God can use these times to not only draw us closer to him but to help lead us toward making necessary decisions—provided we are willing to listen and trust him. That was where I was in May 2016. I needed to trust the Lord, and I needed the help of others. My strong business sense was telling me that it was time to delegate the operations for the commercial company to Mark, who was my director of project management. Mark had been working alongside me for twenty years, and at this point, I needed to lean on him for my sake and the sake of the company. It was the right time and the right place, and I strongly believed that God had led me there. So, Mark became our vice president, director of operations for Derrick Commercial Contracting, and I continued as president without the burden of the day-to-day operations. I would also continue to provide the leadership and vision needed to keep the company on track. This was a Spirit-led moment as I could not be aware of what was going to happen in the next couple of months, making this a timely and wise decision.

Another IVIg five-day course was ordered for me by Neurology, which I did in late May, and like before, my hands felt much better again. I remember that when I got a chance to golf, I so appreciated that I could feel the grip of the club in my hands. I was enjoying the little things in life. I was also starting to wonder how long this was going to go on. Even though I thought that we were working toward some kind of remission, Jeanne and I were beginning to wonder whether that would happen and perhaps some sort of treatment was what I could expect for the rest of my life. Again, I reminded myself that I couldn't control what would happen in the future, but I needed to continue to keep that smile on my face, because I was being taken care of by what I believed were some of the best in the medical field.

The first day of June came, and the new blood test results were not encouraging. My M-spike and related tests for myeloma were up. I would start on the increased dosage of 25 mg of Revlimid in a couple of days, and hopefully that would stabilize my cancer. In the meantime, we talked about this being a good time to have my stem cells harvested for a potential future stem cell transplant. Dr. Gertz recommended that we harvest enough for two transplants, but Jeanne encouraged him to harvest enough for three, considering my young age. Even though Dr. Gertz wasn't necessarily keen on her suggestion, he liked her logic and especially liked it when she said that if we didn't need the third batch of stem cells, we could donate it to scientific research someday. I was very proud of Jeanne for going to bat for me on this, and I was pleased that she was so convinced of my future longevity. He agreed with three, and I started doing another series of tests over the next couple of weeks to make sure that I was healthy enough for the procedure and a potential future transplant. Meanwhile, the 25 mg of Revlimid was driving me nuts! I had a rash covering a large portion of my abdomen and my back. Hematology asked me to suspend the Revlimid to see if it would clear up, which it started to after a few days. Then I was back on the Revlimid and, of course, the rash came back. We also spent a couple of days at Mayo doing a barrage of tests before stem cell harvesting.

After the tests were complete, we had a consultation to go over the results of the tests with Dr. Gertz. He came into the room, which included a couple of other nurses and assistants, greeted Jeanne and me in his normal polite manner, and started by asking to see my rash. As I pulled up my shirt, he looked at the rash and said that it looked uncomfortable and asked if it bothered me. I sarcastically quipped back with a "What do you think?" Then we sat down, and he leaned back in his chair. I'd seen that expression before. He recommended that we come down to Mayo in early July for stem cell harvesting and go right into a stem cell transplant. I think we both said no at the same time, not believing what we were hearing. We had always thought that a stem cell transplant was more of a last resort when other treatments weren't working. Surely there were other treatments they could use before throwing the kitchen sink at me! Dr. Gertz explained that recent studies have shown that doing a stem cell treatment earlier in the treatment process, especially when the patient is healthy, which I was except for this darn rash, resulted in a more durable result from the transplant. He could see that we were quite shocked by his recommendation and said to take a week to think about it, talk it over, and talk to others, like in our MM support group back home. He then ended by saying that we already had an appointment with him next week and there would be no tests or examinations—come to the appointment, and we'd just talk.

That next week was one of turmoil for us. This was a major medical decision. Not only did we pray and pray for discernment, but we also talked about this with as many people as possible who had either gone through this or knew someone who did. Finally, Jeanne called a longtime friend of the family who was an oncologist in San Diego and explained my situation. She told him that the procedure would be at Mayo Clinic. He said that Mayo had some of the top doctors for treating multiple myeloma and that Dr. Gertz was one of them. He recommended we do what Dr. Gertz wanted us to do. This helped with our decision-making, but it was still a tough week.

The next Monday, Jeanne and I were again at Mayo for our appointment with Dr. Gertz. We also brought along our daughter Shelby, who was in the Doctor of Pharmacy program at Drake

University, so she could hear our discussion. Jeanne and I, over that last week with our research and discussion with others, had pretty much decided that if this is what Dr. Getz thought I should do, then we should probably do it. Dr. Gertz came in by himself and sat in his rolling chair, and we introduced him to Shelby, who sat between us on the couch in his exam room. He rolled over to Shelby and faced her and said, "Let me tell you about your father." He proceeded to tell her about all the difficult and bad things that I had gone through. I tried to say that it wasn't so bad, but he was hearing none of it. He explained how hard the treatment had been on me and that the toxicity of the treatment scared him. It was time for a stem cell transplant, and even though it might be rough on me for a couple of months, it gave me what he believed was my best chance for a good long-term prognosis going forward. The compassion with which Dr. Gertz spoke to us that day brought tears to my eyes, as I once again realized that God had given me a very special doctor who not only was extremely good at his profession but also, and perhaps most importantly, really, really cared for his patients and their families. We were truly blessed.

So, it was on to the next journey of 2016. A stem cell transplant. I knew what the procedure was but for some reason, I'd always dismissed the thought that I would go through the process myself. I can't say that I was looking forward to it, but now it was the next necessary journey in this storm. Jeanne and I were in another time of calm, but it would be brief.

CHAPTER 12:

Stem Cell Transplant: Down and Out and Back Again

R eflecting back, the business and financial crisis during the Great Recession didn't seem to be the storm that I thought it was. Yes, it looked dire at the time, and business survival seemed bleak at times. But after the winds of the storm subsided, I came to understand that life is ever-changing and that these storms, however severe, have a way of changing you and your outlook on life. For me, I was better able to see God working in my life, helping me get through this hard time as I learned to trust him. But that storm turned out to be just the prelude to the one-two punch of being diagnosed with incurable cancer and receiving radiation and chemotherapy that really rocked my physical well-being. Now I'd found out that these treatments were not enough. I don't want to pretend to know what God was thinking, but it certainly seemed that he had me where he wanted me, at least where I needed to be, which was more submissive to him and his will for me. All my planning about how my life should go at this stage seemed to no longer matter as I worked my way through this current storm and tried to make sense of what God wanted from me. I was learning that he put me on this earth to serve him and to serve others through the skills and successes he had blessed me with. But first, another and quite possibly the hardest of all the trials lay before me. A stem cell transplant!

We had less than three weeks to prepare for our lives to be interrupted by this procedure. I would be out of the office for approximately four months for the procedure and recovery. We would spend about one month in Rochester, and then recovery would continue at home. However, we were told to be prepared to spend up to one hundred days in Rochester in case of complications. At work, I started my "while I am gone" list, as I was told by my Mayo care team that this would not be a working "vacation." Appointing Mark as director of operations for the commercial company a month prior turned out to be a wise and timely decision because he had had time to embrace and transition into his new position. Our commercial company was on its way to a record year, and I was confident that he and the team would successfully see it through. We had some real estate refinancing that needed to be completed in the next few months, but that process was put in motion before I left, and the closing would happen while I was gone. Ron and Mike certainly had control of the residential operations, which were continuing to improve and grow back from the recession. Tom would watch out for any administrative and operational items that needed attention in addition to his regular responsibilities of managing our field operations. Yes, four months was going to be a long time to be gone, but I would have to let go and let the team do the job that they were so capable of doing. I was confident that we would do well but perhaps was fearful that they would not really miss me and would "do just fine without me." Everyone wants to be wanted and needed, but I was giving up control and leadership for the next four months. I spent those few weeks preparing the best I could, as the higher priority had to be my health.

Jeanne and I prepped for this major medical procedure by learning everything we could from reading, watching videos, and talking to others who had been through it. I called my friend Mike, who I talked about earlier, and he filled me in on the details of his experience. His firsthand experience was very helpful. I was also very grateful for the time that I had been able to spend with Kirk before he passed away and for the substantial information he passed on to me.

I can't give enough credit to Jeanne for working out the many details that were necessary. We decided to stay at the Gift of Life Transplant House just a few blocks away from Mayo Clinic during this procedure. We packed knowing that we were moving to Rochester for at least four weeks and perhaps up to a hundred days. Our new home away from home. Word got around the neighborhood about my serious condition and the upcoming transplant, which prompted the neighborhood women to have a prayer meeting with Jeanne, and she brought back two prayer shawls for me to use while I was recovering. It was very touching to know the care and the prayers that were being showered on us.

We spent the Fourth of July weekend at our cabin with our children and grandchildren. We took time to discuss the procedure that I was about to go through and why. There were many questions that ranged from, when would I lose my hair to what happens if the procedure doesn't work. It was a surreal and anxious time for our family. We were relying on God's Word in Jeremiah 29:11: "For I know the plans I have for you . . . plans to prosper you and not to harm you, plans to give you hope and a future." When we left the cabin at the end of the weekend, reality was settling in that I would probably not be back until Labor Day weekend at the earliest!

We finished our packing and double-checked all our lists, and we were off to Rochester. We checked into the Gift of Life House and were given a room on the lower level. Two beds, a closet and dresser drawers, and our own bathroom. Certainly, very adequate. We shared a communal kitchen and had our own spot in the refrigerator, freezer, and pantry for our food. It was a great arrangement for helping us get to know the patients and their caregivers who were staying there. We all had something in common, either a stem cell or organ transplant.

A stem cell transplant is analogous to a garden that is full of weeds and instead of trying to kill just the weeds, you spray the whole garden with weed and grass killer, killing everything, including your garden plants. After a few days, you replant your garden. Before my transplant could happen, my stem cells needed to be harvested as I was having what is called an *autologous stem cell transplant*, in that I could use my stem cells. Not all blood cancers can be treated this way and many need donor stem cells. I did not have to worry about a match as my stem cells would be harvested, stored, and reused. To start this process, I was given two-a-day injections of a drug called Neupogen, which promoted the overproduction of stem cells in my bone marrow, causing them to be released into my blood system. My first injection was on the Friday after we arrived and continued right through the weekend. Like everything related to cancer treatment, there are always side effects, and for me, it meant lower back spasms, achiness in my legs, headaches, and exhaustion. I just kept telling myself that this was what had to be done, and that even though I was hurting a little, I just needed to keep my eye on the big picture. On Saturday evening we went to a local church service to get our minds focused, knowing what lay ahead, and to ask God for care and protection. We left a note saying why we were in Rochester, asking for prayers, and afterward stayed for the Saturday evening meal that they shared with visitors. We were very appreciative of the hospitality and well wishes that were extended to us.

Monday was a big day, as I had an early morning check-in at the hospital for surgery to have a catheter inserted into a vein in my upper right chest with two ports that came through my skin. This would be used for infusions, blood draws, and harvesting of my stem cells starting the next day. When I awoke from surgery, I was bandaged and stitched up, and after a couple of hours of observation, I was released. Jeanne and I were taught about how to care for the port and how to change the dressing, which seemed like a big responsibility. I was glad that she took good notes and paid attention. We were taught about the importance of drinking lots of fluids and eating healthily during this time and, most importantly, about avoiding infections. This meant not using a toothbrush for cleaning my teeth and no shaving, among other things.

Tuesday was the first day of stem cell harvesting, with a seven a.m. check-in at the Apheresis Unit in the Charlton Building. The stem cell harvesting would last until noon and be repeated daily until they harvested the correct number of stem cells. I was assigned a bed in one of the pods, and they hooked up two tubes to my port. One tube would take the blood out and into a machine next to my bed that used a centrifuge to remove my stem cells, and the other tube would return the remaining blood to my vein. This machine is certainly a miracle of modern medicine! After the stem cells were collected in the bag, they would be frozen for future use. As they needed approximately

3 million stem cells per transplant, my goal was to collect 9 million total, allowing for the ability to have two additional future transplants. Judy was the name of our nurse, and she was a "stitch" in that she could always make us smile or laugh with her one liners. We tried to press her on what to expect from this procedure, and she just said that we are all like snowflakes as no two are alike, just take it as it comes. Wise advice, don't you think? Then the nicest surprise happened, as we got a visit from Susie, the visitation minister from the church we'd attended on Saturday. We had a very nice time together, and it ended with us holding hands as she prayed for a successful transplant and that Jeanne would have the strength to be the caregiver I needed during this time and going forward. It just seemed that every place I looked, God had his hand in my life and was taking care of me through the hands of others. What peace that brought to me. It was a powerful moment that was witnessed by the nurses and other patients on the floor.

Later that day we got a call from the nurse telling us the official count of stem cells harvested. It was a great day at 4.2 million cells, meaning we would be back the next day with a goal of 5 million more! The harvesting procedure was quite routine the next day—same place, same bed. During the morning, however, a surgical team was called in because I started bleeding around my central line. A little Novocain, a couple of stitches, and some fresh bandages fixed me up at least until I was done that morning. However, as I went to leave, there was more blood staining my shirt. One of the nurses put me in a wheelchair and wheeled me down the long hallway into the Eisenberg Methodist Hospital building. At the end of the hallway was Station 94, the best friend of a stem cell transplant patient. We would be visiting there at least once a day for checkups once the transplant started. The double doors opened and closed behind me, and I was put in a room where I received more stitches. Later that day we received the good news that they had harvested an additional 6 million stem cells, meaning we had reached our goal in just two days. What an overachiever, huh? That meant that Thursday would be a rest day before my final checkups and appointments on Friday. One of the to-dos was to get a haircut to prepare for the inevitable: losing my hair. I told the nice gal to use a number 2 and give me a buzz cut. That was another first for me of many firsts happening in my life at this time.

Friday included a few checkups, with the final one being with Dr. Gertz, who gave me the go-ahead for the transplant. I would be the 2,138th stem cell transplant at Mayo Clinic. We were ready.

Early Saturday morning we checked into Station 94. I was given a room and my vitals were checked. After that, my line was hooked up to an IV of saline solution to make sure I was well hydrated. After a couple of hours, they brought in the drug: melphalan (the weed and grass killer). This would be administered to me through my central line for the next hour. While this was happening, I sucked on crushed ice to keep my mouth cold to help prevent mouth sores from forming from the killer chemo drug I was receiving. My white blood count would start going down from here for approximately the next ten days. After receiving the chemo I started another IV of saline solution, and by noon I was dismissed. From this point on though, because of my soon-to-be declining immunity, I would be wearing my N95 face mask in public unless I was in Station 94, my room at Gift of Life, or if I was eating or drinking.

My job now was to eat healthily, drink plenty of fluids, keep moving and walking, and to avoid getting sick. It was Jeanne's job as my caretaker to make sure I did and that I took all medications prescribed throughout the process. Every day also began with going to Station 94 for blood tests and a thorough checkup of my vital signs.

Two days after receiving the melphalan, I was back at Station 94 for the transplant of my stem cells. This was considered day zero of my transplant. The date, July 18, is also considered my "new birthday," as it is the day I received my new blood cells. I was still feeling pretty good at this point, but time would take care of that. My frozen stem cells, that had been harvested the previous week, were securely brought to just outside my room, and the identification tags were carefully checked with my identification band. They were then thawed, brought into the room, and hooked up to one of my ports as I received saline solution and my stem cells simultaneously. The whole process took the better part of the morning but from here on out we began the waiting game. We would watch my white blood cell count continue to go down until it bottomed out and then start to rise. This would be an important milestone as this is the *engraftment stage*, when the transplanted stem cells are starting to make new healthy blood cells. This would probably happen sometime around plus or minus day 10 of my transplant.

Here is where I tell you that my positive attitude carried me through this time with flying colors and without any issues. Unfortunately, my physical state was hurting, and mind over matter was very difficult. I felt nauseous much of the time and, therefore, eating was extremely difficult. Jeanne took me to Station 94 every evening for an infusion of a drug to help with nausea. That would help me go to sleep without the worry of getting sick during the night, and I would usually wake up feeling okay. But as the day went on, the nauseous feeling was almost certain to grow. My taste buds started to play tricks on me too. Food tasted bland, and Jeanne struggled to find food that I would feel like consuming. She also pushed me to increase my fluid intake, and I carried a large drinking cup around the house during the day as a gentle reminder. One day she confronted me, saying that I needed to drink more water, and I answered by telling her that I didn't like the taste of water. Hard to believe but true. My taste buds were temporarily shot. I felt bad that I was so grumpy about this with her, because she worked hard to find something that I might enjoy enough to keep hydrated. She tried a number of other things, but my most popular drink ended up being root beer or orange soda, especially with a scoop of ice cream in it. I could get my calories and fluid at the same time!

Many of my days were spent in a fog. I tried not to nap too much during the day as I wanted to be able to sleep at night.

Much of my time was spent sitting in one of the many living rooms in this old house watching the 2016 Summer Olympics. Again, I couldn't tell you much of what I watched, but it helped me to stay occupied and I also had an opportunity to spend time with others while they healed from their transplants. Sometimes I would sit outside on the covered porch, trying to enjoy the hot, humid summer air. I would usually see Al out there who had his transplant the same day I did and seemed to be doing much better than me. I tried to remember Judy's snowflake comparison, but at this point I just didn't care! I was hurting! During this time Jeanne would go for long walks in Rochester and come back telling me about the neat things she'd seen, as if I would remember. She took me on short walks, especially in the morning, when we walked to the clinic for my daily exam at Station 94. However, at the "low" point, when that became impossible, I would ask her to drive me to the clinic and drop me off, and then I would wait for her before going up to Station 94. It was not an easy time, but I avoided having to be admitted to the hospital even though we were told that about 50 percent of patients are admitted at some point during this procedure.

We had a few visits from friends and family, but because of my foggy state, Jeanne appreciated the visits more than I did. In fact, I had to be reminded sometime later that I'd had visitors, as my mind just was not functioning the way it normally would. Jeanne especially appreciated the visits from Shelby's good friend Joelle, who was a nurse at Mayo Clinic. She came quite often to spend time and play games with Jeanne. I normally sat and watched in a dazed state.

When Jeanne and I first arrived in Rochester, we decided to start a CaringBridge page so that we could more easily communicate with our family and friends about what was happening. I was very hesitant at first because I wasn't sure that I wanted to share this much detail with the "world." Remember, we had kept my cancer very private for a long period but that wasn't the case any longer. I am so glad we started using CaringBridge, and it proved to be a blessing for us as we enjoyed the wonderful comments and well wishes we received from everyone. It was also a way for us to communicate how God had his hand in what was going on and for our followers to offer support and prayers for us. This was an opportunity to use my circumstances to inspire and potentially help others. Every now and then it is nice to go back and review some of our posts and some of the comments, but not too often.

During my transplant time I also found out that a good friend of mine, Jeff, had to have emergency heart surgery. It may be hard to believe but I felt like I was very fortunate to only be going through a stem cell transplant. My empathy for the storms and crises that others were experiencing had certainly deepened. I realized that I could no longer be a bystander, as concern for others was becoming a priority for me, much more so than before my series of storms began. I have found during my journey that I often find others who have something that seems worse than my situation, and it helps remind me to be grateful no matter what my circumstances may be. A reminder that we all get a chance to experience storms in various degrees during our time here on Earth.

On days 11 and 12, I realized that this was a slow process that couldn't be rushed. My temperature was well above normal, but cultures showed that there was no infection, for which we were very thankful. But I still felt lousy—I mean lousy! I was getting IVs of antibiotics, potassium, and saline solution for additional hydration. My body was working hard, and as Jeanne said, my body was like a factory that had a bunch of work to do and was working hard to do it! I seemed to be in two-feet-forward and one-foot-back mode at this point. By day 15 my blood count numbers were climbing rapidly, and I was doing better, relatively speaking! I was exhausted and fatigued, and I depended on Jeanne's help in many ways and spent each day leaning on God for his help. The end was in sight but still seemed a long way off. Certainly the end for my hair had arrived, as I was sporting a new bald look and saw it as my badge of honor!

Finally, on day 17 since my transplant, I had recovered enough to be released. I had my last appointment at Station 94 in the morning and in the afternoon my central line was removed. And may I say good riddance! Even though I had my final checkup and was officially released the next day, I was still feeling about as bad as I had when this journey started back in early July. But I had survived, and Dr. Gertz was happy with my preliminary numbers. Now it was time for the long healing process until I would return on October 31 for my 100-day checkup. While having another five-day IVIg treatment for the recurring neuropathy in my right hand and foot, we stayed in Rochester for almost another week before heading home. I once again appreciated having the feeling back in my hands and feet. What a blessing it was having this treatment that took away most of the neuropathy. The extra time also allowed us to have a luncheon celebration with a few of the couples who went through the stem cell transplant with us at the same time. Again, be grateful for the little things.

In my brokenness during this time, God healed me and helped me to put my trust in him for a positive outcome. He had been very good to me, and his protection and healing have been very evident. While pondering what lay ahead, I realized that I was very blessed. I may have been knocked down again, but with God's help, I was coming back!

CHAPTER 13:

Healing and Reflection

*"I sought the Lord, and he answered me; he delivered
me from all my fears."*

Psalms 34:4

ome, finally, after spending about a month in Rochester for the stem cell transplant and the recovery. I was still not out of the woods as nausea continued to haunt me, and I struggled to keep Jeanne's home cooking down on occasion. But I was home and that felt so good. I spent much of my time on my favorite leather recliner with my maroon and gold Minnesota Gopher fleece blanket over me, just wanting to be comfortable. I also spent time reading the good wishes on CaringBridge, texts, emails, and cards. I continued to feel well loved and well cared for. I was so grateful for all the prayers being showered my way. And, of course, Jeanne was there to take care of me as needed.

During this time, I had a unique understanding that I was in a period of physical, mental, and spiritual healing. I realized that God had given me this time to reflect on what had happened during the last few years and how it had changed me and my attitude. It was as if God was telling me that, since I had been too busy to take the time to examine his purpose for me, he was going to give me that time, and that I needed to use it wisely. In addition to a lot of reading, I started to write "my story" of the last several years. I wasn't sure why I was doing this, but it seemed to me that I should be doing this. I started to spend more time reflecting on the scriptures and continued to journal on how they applied to me and what I was going through. I printed out Psalm 25 and put it on the refrigerator door to constantly remind me. "Guide me in your truth and teach me, for you are God my Savior, and my hope is in you all day long" (verse 5). "Guard my life and rescue me; do not let me be put to shame, for I take refuge in you" (verse 20). These were two of many verses of the Bible that comforted me as I took the time to reflect on my life and the deliverance from my cancer that God was granting me. I truly trusted in him as my faith deepened, and I put my hope in him for my healing.

Physically, I slowly started to overcome the nauseous feeling, and at Jeanne's urging, it was time to start regaining my physical strength and do daily walks. It started with a walk to the end of the driveway to get the mail. Then it was half a block and back. Eventually, I was able to build up my strength and stamina to walk to the end of our neighborhood and back, which was almost a mile. Bill was coming back but it was "New Bill!" I started using this newfound strength to get together with friends to walk and perhaps enjoy lunch together after our walk. I enjoyed the fellowship with others that I had been missing the past few months. My most important and valued walks were with my loving wife, Jeanne, who was with me every step of the way through this storm.

Before knowing that I was going to have a stem cell transplant, I had been asked by Amanda, the executive director of NACDB, to say a few words about what I had been through at the next annual meeting in Arlington, Texas, in late September. After the transplant, I contacted Amanda and told her that I couldn't promise her I would be there. She said that she would list my spot at the end of the day simply as a guest speaker. She told me I could have as much time as I wanted, as she had faith that not only would I be there but that my speech could be the highlight of the day. Talk about pressure!

It was time to go to work on the speech because this gave me purpose as I healed. God had given me the ability to speak in public and now he had given me the story, which I named "Restored by the Storm." The outline of that first speech, unbeknownst to me, was going to be the start of the outline of this book. It was becoming the story of how God drew me closer to him through pain and suffering. It was a speech about not only my financial and health storms but also how I had learned from them to lean on and trust in God no matter what the cir-cumstance. I believed that if God wanted me to be in Arlington for that speech, he would make sure I was there. My job was to reflect on what had happened and put together a speech that would teach and inspire while giving glory to God.

My doctors permitted me to fly to Dallas to give my speech just barely two months after my transplant. I was healing quickly and with purpose. I had spoken in public before, but this was going to be much different from a formal business speech . . . this was going to be my story! Jeanne, of course, flew down with me to be by my side and to be at least one smiling face in the audience that I could count on. The day was filled with great information, sandwiched around a keynote speech by a former Dallas Cowboy, but I kept thinking about the words that I was going to say at the end of the day. Would my words be accepted? Would my delivery be good? Why had I agreed to do this?

When my time came at the end of the day, Amanda politely and confidently introduced me as the highlight of the day. I proceeded to the stage, bald head and all. I said a quick prayer under my breath, stared at the audience, and began: "This is the story of how my faith has moved from my head to my heart." The words kept coming off the outline I had in front of me as I told of how I had been humbled and how God had protected me. As I looked out in the audience, every eye was contacting mine. No one was distracted by their phone or anything else. I believe I had what is referred to as a captivated audience. And, of course, Jeanne was in the middle of the room with her encouraging and beautiful smile. As I finished my speech and left the stage, I simultaneously realized how relieved and exhausted I was. All I could say was thank you, God!

Then a most miraculous thing happened after Amanda closed the conference. A group of attendees, many of whom I knew, approached me and asked if they could pray for me and my healing from cancer. I don't know how many were gathered around me as all I could do was look down while the tears flowed from my eyes. I don't know if I have ever experienced a public display of caring and praying as I did that day.

Between 2016 and 2019, before the pandemic, I had several more opportunities to tell my story to many different small and large groups. I quickly learned that my story could help others by encouraging them that no matter what their situation or storm, they could get through it and to trust God along the way. I always try to think about those one or two hearts that I might be speaking to when on stage and hope that my words will inspire and help them in some way.

On October 31, I was at Mayo Clinic for my 100-day checkup and blood tests. I had gained back most of the weight I had lost, and I was now sporting a nice head of "peach fuzz." I was feeling very well and was anxious to hear the results of my tests. Dr. Gertz greeted us as he came into the room and immediately sat down in front of the computer screen. After a brief review, he said that he was very pleased with the results and that my M-spike was at a very acceptable level, and as long as it stayed near that level, he would consider the procedure a success. Of course, there were no questions as to how long I could expect to remain in this near-remission state. All that was certain was my current status, and we would take it month by month for the time being. He did disappoint us, though, when he recommended that I once again start taking the chemotherapy drug Revlimid as a "maintenance" drug, as studies showed that transplant patients have a more durable and longer-lasting recovery when taking a maintenance drug. This caught us off guard as I had not anticipated being on chemo after the transplant. But if it would help in the long-term success of the vicious procedure I'd gone through, we thought it was best to follow the advice of my doctor, of whom we thought so highly. So, it has been twenty-one days on with seven days off ever since.

It was also at this appointment that I asked Dr. Gertz if I should go back to work as I am trying to keep my priorities where they should be. He asked me if I enjoyed my work, to which I responded, "Most of it." (Not sure why that came out of my mouth, but it did.) His advice was to do what I enjoyed and delegate the other duties. Seemed like not only sound medical advice but great business advice also. I was fortunate to be in a position where I could do that, so back to work I went after being on a four-month sabbatical!

Even though I had visited the office a couple of times during my recovery and had started making a few business calls while at home, it did feel strange going back to the office for that first day of work. It seemed like I had to reacquaint myself with everyone once again and to get up to speed with what happened while I was gone. One of my brothers poked his head into my office and informed me that he was glad I was back and that he did not want my job, nor would he ever question what I did again! It was a blessing to hear that, but I also understood the additional pressure he had taken on in my absence. I was blessed to have partners and staff who would allow me the time that I needed to recover. I was coming back with a renewed and grateful spirit. I was determined to no longer stress out over the small things and to be willing to listen more intently and delegate more to others. Most importantly, I was also determined that I would do my best to trust in God for all things going forward. While it may not be easy to do sometimes, it was something that needed to be done if he was truly going to be driving. I had promised him this while I was on the radiation table.

Our business had turned the corner. The years 2016 and 2017 were very good for our commercial construction company and our residential company was steadily growing. We had transitioned from survival mode to thriving mode. Having had to work through the tough times of the Great Recession and the crisis that it brought upon us, I enjoyed the time of prosperity we were entering but I wouldn't take it for granted. It was with an attitude of gratitude that I approached each and every day. I knew where our blessings came from and would be thankful for what we had.

On July 18, 2017, I celebrated the one-year "birthday" of my transplant. Jeanne invited everyone, and I do mean everyone, that we knew to our party. I believe it was bigger than any birthday party I have ever had. There were so many people there who just wanted to say hi and wish Jeanne and me the best, with thankfulness that I had weathered the storm of the transplant. They were proud I was doing my best to kick cancer, and I don't think I have ever felt so much love from so many people at any one time. I didn't want the night to end as it was a wonderful night of celebration!

At the end of January 2018, our mother, Mary Ann, finally succumbed to her hideous Alzheimer's disease and went home to be with her Savior. I was given the honor to deliver the eulogy for her, remembering the woman who raised five successful children and worked side by side with her husband to start and grow a successful family business. She was always a servant to anyone who needed her. She was quite a lady, and it was sad to see her liveliness destroyed by her illness. Six months later, Dad died. We know that he had congestive heart disease, but we believe that he died of a broken heart. It was my honor once again to deliver the eulogy, remembering a wonderful husband, father, and leader who left behind a great legacy for not only his family but also the community that he lived in for most of his life. Two larger-than-life examples for me to follow.

Shortly after Mom's death, Jeanne and I took a dream trip to Israel and Palestine and stood in the places where Old Testament leaders once stood. We stayed three nights in Bethlehem right across the square from the Church of the Nativity, marking the spot where Jesus was born in a stable. We went to many places where Jesus had journeyed. We went to the mountaintop stronghold of Masada that overlooked the Dead Sea and, later in the day, floated in the very buoyant, salty water. We spent time hiking in the Ein Gedi, wondering which caves along this canyon had been inhabited by David and his men while fleeing from Saul. We went north, south, east, and west, learning all about the people and the geography of the areas we visited. We used the Bible as our guide and saw where David slew Goliath, and we went to the wilderness where the Israelites spent forty years before entering the Promised Land. We saw the ruins of the village where Jacob lived. We went north of the Sea of Galilee to Caesarea Philippi where Peter declared that Jesus was the Messiah. We spent time in the towns along the Sea of Galilee where Jesus first recruited his disciples. You get the idea—we saw it all. Then we went to Jerusalem. We walked from one end of Hezekiah's Tunnel to the other end. We saw the excavation for the City of David. We visited museums, churches, and ancient pools that were used in Jesus's time. We went to the Mount of Olives and followed Jesus's route to Jerusalem on Palm Sunday. We went to the Garden of Gethsemane where Jesus was arrested, and we went to the traditional place where Jesus was crucified and buried as well as to the Church of the Holy Sepulchre, which most believe was built over the actual area where he was crucified and buried. It really doesn't matter where he was crucified and buried because regardless of where that happened, the tomb was empty on Easter morning. He suffered death for our sins and conquered death for us.

On our last day of the trip, we went to the Western Wall in Jerusalem, with the men to one side and the women separated by a wall to the other side. I did as everyone does and took a small sheet of paper and wrote my prayers on the paper, folded it up several times, and stuffed it into one of the cracks in the wall. My two prayers were these: (1) healing from my cancer, and (2) the ability to better understand what God wants me to do going forward. I then put my hand on the wall. It was a beautiful, sunny, 70-degree February day in Jerusalem, and I can tell you that my hand felt like it was "magnetically" stuck to the wall as I prayed. What I heard was, "I will take care of your health; you just listen to me and do what I ask." I really have no other way to explain this experience. It was real to me and was the highlight of my travels in the Promised Land. It certainly gave me something to think about on our long flight home.

We had my normal monthly checkup at Mayo Clinic the week after we returned from Israel. Up to this point our appointments had been routine, with my M-spike staying in that range they wanted. This appointment was routine again, but a day later I noticed that there wasn't an Mspike on my blood report. I waited until the next month and asked why they didn't measure my M-spike and was told that they still do but that now it was not measurable. We were told that this can happen on a rare occasion but that it will probably come back within a few months. It is now 2024, some six years later as I finish this book, and my medical report still says, "Abnormality present but unmeasurable." Do you believe that God is still working miracles today? I do. I believe that we just need to open our eyes and watch for how God is working in our lives. I was told when diagnosed that the average life expectancy was seven years from diagnosis, and it is now over ten years later and the bottom of my reports says, "Patient in remission and doing remarkably well." I realize that our storms in life don't always end the *way* we want nor *when* we want them to. Some of our storms will leave us with unwanted, lifelong changes. They all don't have a happy ending. I deal with neuropathy in my feet and hands as well as other side effects from the chemotherapy that I have had and still take to this day. I certainly am aware that the myeloma can come back at any time, but in the meantime, I will gladly proclaim what God has done for me. He has taken me through two major storms in my life and has brought me to the other side so that I am, in many ways, a much better person than I was before the storm. He has restored me.

CHAPTER 14:

Restored

After a wonderful day at the cabin, one of my grandsons, as he walked away from the evening campfire to go to bed, said, "It's been a great day." He got it. Understanding gratitude each and every day, even in the small things, is a wonderful gift. Not everything will go your way on any given day, but starting and ending each day with an "attitude of gratitude," as Zig Ziglar used to say, can make each day special.

I start this final chapter with that thought. *Gratitude*. As I have experienced the storms of life that came my way, I have learned the importance of being grateful and not taking my blessings and gifts in life for granted. Instead of the feeling of "look what I have," perhaps gratitude and thankfulness for what you have will work better. Take each day as it comes, showing gratitude every day. Yes, be grateful for all your blessings, whatever they may be. Then use those blessings to bless others. When you receive that compliment, say thank you and don't shrug it off. Be that person whose attitude lights up the room when you enter it, not when you leave it. Employ the Golden Rule by showing respect to others as you would want to be respected. Do not act like the universe revolves around you. It's important to be grateful even when everything seems wrong or off. Be grateful that God is there for you during those times and will help calm the storm and carry you through. Can we be grateful during times of need as well as times of plenty?

I have been restored while traveling through the storms that I have detailed in the previous chapters. It is important to understand and learn from the different seasons of life that come to us. These seasons are not always good but are not always bad either. When bad things happen, it is natural to ask the question, "Where is God?" God is there waiting for us to lean into him whether the eye of the storm is at our doorstep or if it has passed. To survive, we need to learn from these storms by drawing ourselves closer to God. He is there for us in the storm as well as the sunshine. We are all going to experience storms in our lives, and we have a choice about how we respond to them instead of just being defined by them.

Watch for and be ready for those life-changing moments in your life. These are moments in time when God works events and circumstances to help us on our way through life. In early November 2019, I was invited to participate in a "Leadership

& Legacy" (L&L) group with a small group of businessmen from around the country. I was invited to this by Bryan Dodge, author, public speaker, and business consultant. Three days were spent learning and helping each other to improve our leadership skills so that, in turn, we can make our part of the world a better place and thus build a legacy. At the latter part of the three days, I had a chance to share with the group why I had spent the time and money to attend this event. I had just turned sixty-five, and I was starting to explore what might be next for me. When Bryan heard that he asked, "What does that mean? Have you finished what you started?" He and the others in this group helped me see that a lot of people depended on me to continue to help lead the charge at our company. I came back from that time fired up and wearing an imaginary T-shirt that said, "Bill's back." I was refreshed and revived and recommitted myself to lead the charge at Derrick Companies. Today I still enjoy what I am doing as I help prepare our company for the next generation of leadership, confident that God will let me know when it is time for "what's next." As I was preparing last summer to go to the L&L reunion in Bozeman, Montana, my son Michael said that he remembered when I came back from that meeting in 2019. He said that I was "fired up" and saw it as one of those life-changing moments in my life. Michael and I started to think about what might have changed if I hadn't gone. I may have retired and perhaps Michael, who started working with us last year, may not have come to work for the family business without me there. But I didn't retire, and he is here being trained as one of our future leaders. And without having a friend and coach like Bryan, I may not have written this book. Watch for those life-changing moments when they happen. It is like coming to a fork in the road. We need to choose well. But remember, God puts people in our lives at the right time to help us with those decisions. We need to pay attention.

Based on my experience, you will need a very strong and loving friend to walk with you during your times of trial. For me, that is my wife, Jeanne, who has been with me every step of the way as I grappled with the effects of our financial struggles and, more importantly, as my caregiver while we fought cancer together. She was the advocate I needed, writing down every note and every instruction from every medical meeting and medical test. She waited with me in the waiting rooms before and during every scan and procedure that I had. She sat beside me praying and comforting me during all the months of infusions. And she helped keep me going during my stem cell transplant. If you are going through a similar storm, lean on your caregiver, your advocate, whoever that may be. That's why God provided this person for you.

"Many are the plans in a person's heart, but it is the Lord's purpose that prevails" (Proverbs 19:21). I once heard it said, that if you want to make God laugh, just tell him your plans! I heard in a recent sermon that God is looking for us to trust in him without always trying to predict what he wants us to do. When we are going through storms in our lives, it is very hard to know why we go through these rough times. But there is purpose and meaning in these times, only we may not truly understand until we are down the road a way and can look back. If we trust in God, he will show us the reason. There is nothing random about our lives. God is in control, not us. Do it God's way, be patient, and see where he will take you. He is helping you write every chapter of your story. How in the world do you do all this? Through prayer, accepting his Word, fellowship, and having good a relationship with our Lord above. I personally find it very difficult to understand how someone can get through a crisis in life without a strong faith in God.

Choose to face your storms with a great attitude. I have a plaque in my office that I bought at a gift shop in Dublin that reads, "Life isn't about waiting for the storm to pass, it's about learning to dance in the rain." As you face your storms, face them with a great attitude as you deal with your new normal, knowing that you can trust God to get you through. Build your life on solid rock, as Jesus tells us in Matthew 7:24: "Therefore everyone who hears these words of mine and puts them into practice is like a wise man who built his house on the rock." Grit is needed during these times. Don't give up. Don't quit. Lean into God by reading his words in the Scriptures. See how he carried men like Job and Joseph of the Old Testament. Job had everything and lost it all, and even though he questioned why, he remained faithful to God. In the end, God blessed him for his faithfulness and trust. Joseph went through trial after trial but trusted God through it all. God used Joseph's trials to train and prepare him for the future God had in store for him. At God's timing, he was delivered from prison and became a great leader in Egypt, and in doing so, he saved his people from a seven-year drought. There was purpose in their sufferings and there is purpose in our sufferings, even though it is hard to see it during our trials and storms. Know that God will use your sufferings for your good and his ultimate glory. Philippians 4:13 (ESV) states, "I can do all things through him who strengthens me."

It is time for us to stop living our lives like we are going to live forever. We only have one life and a limited amount of time to make the difference in this world that our Lord wants us to make. I don't believe God cares as much about my successes in life as he cares about what I do with that success and the difference that I can make in the lives of others. Some of us may be in the fourth quarter of our lives or close to it. It is never too late to do what you need to do to finish well and to finish strong. Just like in a football game, a lot of action happens in the last quarter and many times it determines the outcome. Is it too much to believe that our greatest work may still be ahead of us?

When you are going through a particularly hard time, you must keep going. Don't let the fear of what you are going through keep you from looking to the future. Understand that going through the storm is a time of preparation for you. When we are up against these struggles, don't miss the blessings hidden within the struggle. By doing this we can be a light and blessing to others. Others will notice how you handle yourself during those times of struggle. As a business leader, it was tough to not dwell on my circumstances, but with humility and without fear, I needed to move forward, depending on God along the way. People were depending on me to make the right decisions even in my suffering.

I can look back now and see that my storms have been a blessing to me, a wonderful gift. No, I am not saying I'm glad that I have cancer. But what I am saying is that what the storms have taught me and how they have changed me gives me reason to be thankful to God for what he has done for me. He truly prepared me to be a better person and a better leader. I like the new Bill better than the old Bill and I believe God does too.

Whether you are currently in a storm or have come out of one, or even if you have been blessed that you haven't been in a major one yet, live each day on purpose. Try to understand your purpose while you are on this earth and live that way. For the many reasons that I have written above, I have no regret for what has happened to me, because I have learned, or at least I try, to trust in God in all that happens. "For I know the plans I have for you, declares the Lord, plans for good and not for evil, to give you hope and a future" (Jeremiah 29:11). He will bring you through the storm, only it will be in his time, not yours, and his timing will probably be longer than yours (I can almost guarantee that). But good will come. It may not look like you expect, or even want, but you too can be restored by the storm. I have confidence that nothing will break me as I have put my hope in him. That brings peace to me.

One last time. No matter what your circumstances, no matter what your age, no matter your physical or mental situation, no matter how tragic your experience may have been, or what crisis you are facing or have faced, believe and trust in our sovereign Lord, as **THE BEST IS YET TO COME!**

ACKNOWLEDGMENTS

My brothers and business partners, Tom, Ron, and Mike. We have worked well together while using our individual strengths and skills. That, combined with grit and, of course, God's grace, allowed us to survive the Great Recession when others in our industry could not.

With deep gratitude to my medical team at Mayo Clinic, headed by Dr. Morie Gertz. Your knowledge, experience, skills, and care have not only helped me to survive but to thrive.

Bryan Dodge, who one day called me and stated that I had a book in me, and it was time to write it. Thank you for the motivation and resources you provided me to start and finish this book. You are a true friend and trusted adviser.

Thank you, David Williams, for countless hours editing this first book of mine. It has been a pleasure working with you and I truly value your input. Thank you also to Shelli Gustafson for proofreading assistance.

Terry Whalin, acquisitions editor for Morgan James Publishing. Thank you for reading my manuscript and recommending it for publishing. Also, many thanks to the professional and hard-working staff at Morgan James.

To our parents, Bill and Mary Ann, who started our family business in 1967 and taught us the importance of hard work and taking risks. You left us in 2018, but your legacy continues.

To Vince Miller, founder of Resolute and leader of men. Thank you for your wisdom, encouragement, and prodding in the completion of this book.

To my Thursday morning men's group, for your constant prayers and encouragement.

To the bankers, lawyers, and business advisors who came beside me and our business during the cruel time of the recession. You know who you are, and I thank you for your time, help, and understanding.

To all my many friends and neighbors who had a hand in this book with your encouragement, thoughts, and prayers for healing and strength. I would list your names but for fear of forgetting someone.

Finally, thank you, Jeanne. I have been so blessed to be your husband. You listened to me as I cried and vented at night when business was bad. We cried together when the doctor told us that I had cancer. You have always been at my side, praying for me, encouraging me, and acting as my advocate when I was unable to. In you, God has provided me with the best caregiver that I could ever ask for. You also have read and re-read my manuscript more than anyone else and offered much advice along the way. Your detailed notes of our walk with cancer helped me so much as those chapters were being written. This book is so much better because of you and your input.

ABOUT THE AUTHOR

Bill Derrick is an enthusiastic business leader who helped to successfully lead his family's construction and development business through the worst recession since the Great Depression of the 1930s. Using his vast experience, as well as his business and engineering education, he and his partners navigated through a time that threatened the survival of the family's business. Bill is a lifelong learner, who enjoys reading business, motivational, and leadership books. Occasionally, you will catch him reading a nonfiction book or even a novel or two. Bill and his wife, Jeanne, reside just outside the Twin Cities of Minneapolis and St. Paul, Minnesota, in Hudson, Wisconsin. They enjoy spending time with their children and grandchildren as well as traveling the world to far-off places. As an excellent storyteller and keynote public speaker, Bill uses his story to inspire and bring hope to those struggling through life and leaves all with great life lessons, whether they are in a storm or not.

A free ebook edition
is available with the
purchase of this book.

To claim your free ebook edition:

1. Visit MorganJamesBOGO.com
2. Sign your name CLEARLY in the space
3. Complete the form and submit a photo of the entire copyright page
4. You or your friend can download the ebook to your preferred device

Print & Digital Together Forever.

Snap a photo   Free ebook   Read anywhere

Printed in the USA
CPSIA information can be obtained
at www.ICGtesting.com
LVHW050012060924
789769LV00002B/3